Praise

Soul Writing is a fascinating exploration of how to connect with each person's deep internal wisdom. For those who want to tap into inner guidance and the eternal quest for self-discovery, this is a clear, inspiring, and lucid explanation of exactly how to do it. After reading this book, it would be all but impossible to resist taking pen in hand and embarking on the journey of a lifetime . . . or better yet, the journey of multiple lifetimes.

> —**Paul Rademacher, executive director of The Monroe Institute and author of** *A Spiritual Hitchhiker's Guide to the Universe: Travel Tips for the Spiritually Perplexed*

The good news is that Joanne DiMaggio promises to show you a safe, reliable method of contacting your own personal source of wisdom, available on demand. The better news is that she delivers. Some things are easier done than said: *Soul Writing* shows you how it's done, and how *you* can do it.

> —**Frank DeMarco, author of** *The Cosmic Internet*

DiMaggio has been exploring inspirational writing, both as a writer and as a researcher, for years. As an executive member of Edgar Cayce's Association for Research and Enlightenment, she had the opportunity to put her knowledge into practice in many ways. This book is an offshoot of her study and work. One of the first things she wants readers to understand is the difference between inspirational writing and automatic writing. Inspirational writing comes from a divinely connected source within us, she explains. It is not meant to communicate information from an unknown, outside source. It is meant to help the inspired writer peel off layers that obscure the inner wisdom and move the writer to a place of greater insight and comfort. She offers the reader lots of clearly written information, fleshed out with examples from her personal experience, on how to accomplish that goal. She helps readers learn to use inspired writing to explore past lives, enhance psychic abilities, as a tool for psychoanalysis, and for soul growth. Customers who are already journaling will find this one very helpful in moving their writing to the next level.

—**Anna Jedrziewski**
New Age Retailer

Soul Writing

Conversing with Your Higher Self

JOANNE DIMAGGIO, MA

Olde Souls
Press

Cover design by Jane Hagaman
Cover art by iStockPhoto
Author photo by Kalin Scharnbeck/KMS Photography

Quotes from *Channeling Your Higher Self,* © Henry Reed, PhD, 2007.
Used by permission.

Edgar Cayce Readings, copyright ©Edgar Cayce Foundation,
1973, 1993–2009. Used by permission.

Olde Souls Press
P.O. Box 6475
Charlottesville, VA 22906-6475

Production services provided by Quartet Books

If you are unable to order this book from your local
bookseller, you may order directly from the publisher at
www.oldesoulspress.com

Library of Congress Control Number: 2011929240

ISBN 978-0-9836132-0-6

10 9 8 7 6 5 4 3 2 1
Printed on 100% recycled, acid-free paper in Canada

Contents

Foreword

by Henry Reed, PhD

If you've ever had to write a difficult letter, you've probably spent some time preparing yourself mentally. You search for the right opening words, cross out many, then, with a deep breath and a sigh, you begin to write, hoping for the best. Instinctively, you know that what comes out onto the paper is only partially in your control. You instinctively understand that the better frame of mind you have, the better the writing will be. Although you've probably not thought about it as such, you do have an understanding for "inspirational writing."

Taken as a spiritual craft, one can develop such a fine frame of mind that the writing flows out with such inspirational force that it just seems like it's coming from heaven. We have such great spiritual intelligence, invented by our Creator and polished over millennia of human experience. Inside us, there is terrific wisdom just waiting for the correct frame of mind in order to materialize. Just as it's hard to think creatively when you are afraid, so it is easy to imagine the sublime when you are in an inspired mood. Inspirational writing is the easiest way to surprise yourself by discovering all the wisdom that lies dormant within, ready to come out and express itself when it's invited to respond to a pressing need.

This book is an invitation to discover just how wise you are. It is a guidebook to a proven path of spiritual guidance and growth. In my years teaching creativity, intuition, and spirituality, I have found that inspirational writing is the easiest way to demonstrate to someone that they have a higher intelligence, a cosmic creator within. I find *Jonathan Livingston Seagull* to be an example that most folks can relate to. With faith in the possible, we can fly higher and higher, become aware of more and more. We just need to make that leap of faith.

What is that leap? In her book, Joanne DiMaggio describes all the processes involved. There is the leap from setting an intention to letting the pen fly. There is the leap from knowing what it is that you wish to learn to allowing your mind to relax and letting the information rise up spontaneously. There is the leap from making an effort to going with the flow. The practice of inspirational writing then becomes a spiritual practice in trusting Spirit. It allows the practitioner to retire from having oneself as a "job," to let go of the sense of duty to be in command at all times. We discover that there's a flow to life as well. There's a flow to life we can ride, discovering our own inspired responses emerging spontaneously. It teaches you that you can trust life, trust yourself, and find even greater inspiration and joy in living by not trying so hard, but allowing it to be easy. Learning inspirational writing can teach you how to live from inspiration at all times. In that surprising way, this book can actually change your life.

Acknowledgments

In a book whose genesis took more than twenty years, it is a challenge to recall all of the souls who played a significant role in its ultimate publication. To all—on both sides of the veil—who have been part of my journey, I am grateful beyond words. I am especially indebted to:

The Divine Source of the inspiration that continues to illuminate my way.

Amy Betit, for mentoring many of my courses at Atlantic University and whose comments—both personal and professional—encouraged me to persevere.

Bobbie, Cathy, Hilda, Jean, Judy, Maryanne, Poppy, and Vivienne—who turned an interesting research project into a life-changing experience.

Edgar Cayce, my guiding light throughout this project.

Karen Cersley, for her unshakable belief in me and for the awesome logo and website she designed for Olde Souls Press.

Karen Davis at the Edgar Cayce Foundation, for the hours she spent reviewing the quoted Cayce readings for accuracy and for her positive response to the book and to my work.

Frank DeMarco, for our thought-provoking conversations

about writing with "The Guys Upstairs," for his publishing advice, and for his much-appreciated book endorsement.

Cynthia Mitchell, Jane Hagaman, Sara Sgarlat, and Tania Seymour at Quartet Books, for their invaluable help in getting this book published.

Paul Rademacher, for the wonderful book endorsement and for introducing me to the opportunities at The Monroe Institute, which I hope to someday utilize to achieve an even more profound level of writing.

Henry Reed, who first introduced me to inspirational writing during an A.R.E. conference in Chicago. Who would have thought that nearly twenty years later he would be mentoring my culminating project on the same topic? Henry gave me a sense of direction and planted the seed for publication when he said my thesis would make "a great book." Thank you for writing such a masterful foreword.

And, finally, my family, who gave me the space to pursue this project and turn a sixteen-year dream into a reality.

 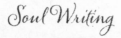

Introduction

Around the age of nine, I decided to create a secret code. I did it not because I was absorbed in stories about Cold War espionage, nor did I have a fascination with mysteries. My motive was pure and simple—revenge.

It was the late 1950s. I was living on the south side of Chicago in a small brick bungalow that my parents, my brother John, and I shared with my maternal grandparents, who had come to the U.S. from their native Sicily at the turn of the twentieth century. They learned to speak what we referred to as "broken English" but always slipped back into their familiar Sicilian dialect whenever they—or my parents—wanted to say something not meant for young ears.

My parents were first-generation Americans but spoke Italian fluently. For reasons they never stated, they opted not to share the gift of the Italian language with my brother or me, so John and I came to view their foreign conversations as an exclusionary tool. This was extremely annoying to me, so to retaliate, I came up with a "language" of my own.

I went into the one private room we had in the house—the bathroom—and sat under the sink drawing figures to create an alphabet known only to me. Even at that early age, I had already developed a fascination for handwriting, so using the pen to create sweeping lines and curves gave me enormous satisfaction.

Once I had my alphabet in place, I used it to write coded messages that I left in strategic places all over the house. I was sure my scraps of paper with their unreadable content would be a source of curiosity for my parents. Perhaps they'd realize what it felt like to be left out in the cold. But my plan backfired. My parents showed no interest whatsoever in my secret code. After a few days, I gave up and never used that alphabet again.

Fast forward some twenty-five years, and I am married with two small children, living the American dream in Naperville, a suburb of Chicago. Still intrigued by the art of handwriting, I enrolled in a calligraphy class at a neighboring community college. The idea of using pen and ink to create elegant letters appealed to me, and I was excited about all the projects in which I could apply this newfound skill. What I didn't anticipate was that I got much more than lessons in "beauty writing," as calligraphy was termed.

The first night of class, the instructor discussed the history of handwriting and put up a chart showing early handwritten marks. To my astonishment, the letters were exact replicas of my childhood alphabet. How in the world could she have known my secret code? Then she revealed its source. It was the Phoenician alphabet, dating back to around 1050 B.C. Somewhere in the ether, that alphabet was floating around, and I happened to tap into it.

That's how inspirational writing—or soul writing, as I prefer to call it—works. You reach into an invisible realm, a higher consciousness, and extract whatever information you seek, and it comes to you in the form of the written word. Special skills, talents, and abilities aren't necessary. It's something everyone can do.

Edgar Cayce (1877–1945), the most documented psychic of the twentieth century and founder of the Association for Research and Enlightenment (A.R.E.), said it is our birthright to communicate with our Source and listen to that still, small voice within our souls—a voice that guides and inspires us to find the answers that lie within. That is the essence of soul writing.

As a transpersonal tool of attunement, soul writing can enrich one's life beyond measure. In the nearly twenty-five years I have practiced inspirational writing, I have witnessed its ability to help myself and others connect with Spirit and discover our divine purpose. Writing from this level helps to clarify earthly goals and esoteric ideals, and its healing quality can have a significant, positive impact on those challenged by physical, emotional, mental, or spiritual issues. When applied to everyday life, soul writing provides profound insights in understanding relationships, finances, careers, and friendships and offers gentle guidance into that yearned-for state of forgiveness. Simply stated, it transforms lives.

While working toward my masters degree in transpersonal studies at Atlantic University, I chose inspirational writing as my thesis. As I began to research this topic, I discovered there was widespread confusion about the definition of inspired writing. I found overlapping descriptions of the processes of "automatic" and "inspirational" writing, with inspirational writing often being misinterpreted as automatic writing and vice versa. This ambiguity, and the fact that there are few books on the market explaining the process of inspirational writing in the spirit of the Cayce readings, led me to develop my research findings as the basis for a book on the subject.

I began by compiling the knowledge I had gained on the subjects of automatic and inspirational writing through personal experience, from lectures, and from available literature.

I wanted to have a firm grasp on all aspects of the topic before enlisting the participation of volunteers for the research portion of the project. In the course of gathering information, I realized that as a stand-alone phrase, "inspirational writing" meant different things to different people.

The terms "inspirational writing" and "automatic writing" are often interchanged because of a lack of understanding that they are two different methods of meditative writing. This innocent mistaking of one for the other has resulted in a widespread misconception about the dynamics of each method. I will explore the difference between the two later, but I wanted to raise this point now because throughout the book many of the people I talk about reference their use of "automatic writing" when in fact they are discussing elements of "inspirational writing."

Soul writing is a form of channeling—a method of communication that accesses information from a Higher Source emanating from one's soul. Some people believe that Source is God. Others credit guardian angels or spirit guides, while still others believe it is higher self or subconscious mind. It doesn't really matter what you call it. In the end, it is a connection to the Infinite—to the All That Is.

Writers have been using the process of inspirational writing for centuries, although not all identified their writing as being connected to a Divine Source. Regardless of what or who you believe is on the other end of your spiritual hotline, the process in and of itself is a fascinating look at how the Creative Forces are available to all of us. It is this process—working together with us as co-creators—that enables us to access information from an invisible world and reach heights unattainable in a conscious state.

The Creative Forces present lessons and guidance for us in ways that best suit us. For me, writing has been a key ele-

ment in many of my incarnations. In some of the past lives I have explored, I have been a scribe; a truth seeker who has observed and recorded events over centuries. Whether I did this for historical purposes, for commercial gain, or simply to keep a private journal, in one way or another, writing has been a part of my spiritual DNA for centuries. So as part of my soul's genetic makeup, it does not surprise me in the least that I receive guidance through the written word.

This is not my secret talent, for every soul communicates with a higher power in its own way. Compared to other forms of meditation, what makes soul writing so unique is that it leaves behind tangible evidence of that connection. The words it brings forth are there to revisit again and again. In a meditative state, images and messages come and go. The strongest ones, the ones that leave the most lasting impression, are those that nudge the soul in some silent way. The person is overcome by a knowing that moves them to action or to a deeper contemplative state through which transformation occurs.

For those who receive guidance in this way, the experience is over in a brief moment. But for those who communicate with Spirit through writing, the experience does not end when the writing stops, for the writing creates a legacy of truth. A treasure chest of comforting and empowering guidance is presented to the writer. That guidance is alive and fluid, growing more relevant as time passes. It is amazing but true. With soul writing, what one records in the moment takes on a totally new meaning as time passes and the soul grows.

The process of soul writing is the same for everyone. What is different from individual to individual is the quality of the message, which is a reflection of the quality of the question, of the intent and ideal of the writer, and of the frequency on which each individual soul operates.

The questions that writers put forth in soul writing sessions make for interesting reading. Some writers ask questions that exclusively pertain to their earthbound existence—the *why* of everything, the *how* of everything, the *when* of everything. From questions about why one is suffering from a particular illness to understanding the pain of a broken heart, these questions are typical of those asked in prayer all the time. Prayer is a powerful tool, and each person who whispers a silent request does so with the hope that an answer will present itself in some mysterious, even miraculous, way.

Yet with soul writing, the answers come forth immediately, and the message is expansive, going beyond the simplicity of the question to a higher understanding. Asking about an illness may bring about an answer that a doctor cannot give, such as what is the root source of the circumstances that brought about the illness in the first place. Was it an abnormality of a cell, or was it karmic in nature?

This deeper knowing of *why* something has happened often has little to do with any answers that may present themselves in one's conscious thoughts. Soul writing creates an entirely new perspective. It opens the eyes of the writer to a new dimension where black-and-white answers are not as obvious. Soul writing gently prompts the writer to look deeper, to peel away the layers of the obvious to reveal the more obscure origins of an issue.

If you are having trouble with your finances, for instance, the source of those problems may not necessarily be because math was never your strongest subject at school. Inspired writing provides the *why* of your woes. It guides you to discover where the problem originated. What circumstances led to the situation you are now in? How is this challenging you? What lesson is there to learn? These questions are raised to enable the writer to see with new eyes, to hear with new ears, to touch the intangible and understand that everything is connected and has a purpose.

Soul writing is a gift that God tucked in our backpacks when we made our journey to Earth. It is our toll-free, phone-home card that has no limits and no expiration date. For me, it is a never-ending source of wisdom and joy. I never feel alone, for guidance is always available to me, no matter what my mood may be, no matter what time of day, no matter where I am. There is a sublime comfort in this knowledge. That is something you, too, can experience when you pick up your pen to journal and then confidently knock on Spirit's door. Someone is always home.

CHAPTER ONE

Writing with the Muse

A study of soul writing is a study in the creative process. All people are creative in one form or another. The question is—do some creative endeavors, by their very nature, dip into a deeper well than others? This question is especially poignant when applied to the creative arts. Many artists, composers, actors, and writers have learned—whether by accident or intentionally—to access an unseen dimension that becomes an endless fountain from which their creative genius flows. They reach that invisible world by entering an altered state of consciousness brought about by trance, meditation, or dreams. While in this altered state, the quality of their work changes to something on a much higher level; different in style, tone, and composition from what they produce in a conscious state.

Artists, writers, and composers who try to capture their process in words struggle with the same questions—what is inspiration, and where does it come from? How am I able to break through the mundane aspects of everyday life, to leave the confines of my physical environment and sail unencumbered to the unlimited heights wherein the Creative Forces await?

Read through the autobiographies and letters of famous artists, writers, and composers, and you will see how each describes a moment of inspiration when they gained an insight that was different from anything they received in a waking state. When in this reverie, elevated to the unconscious storehouse of universal wisdom, they produced extraordinary work.

When describing the writing process, English poet Percy Shelley acknowledged that this heightened level of inspiration comes from beyond the writer's conscious state. But writers aren't the only ones to experience this cosmic high. Great scientists, artists, and inventors all appeal to a Higher Source, a divinity, or some kind of internal "Daemon."

Over many centuries, the role of the Daemon—best described as an attendant or indwelling spirit—in the guided writing process has been cited by countless writers and provides an insight into who or what they considered to be the source of their creative genius.

Rudyard Kipling accessed his inner helper by a form of meditation that he described as "drifting." The first time he experienced this reverie, he felt as though his Daemon came to him, filling him with ideas and instructions to take down the inner dictation he was receiving. Kipling obeyed and eventually learned to recognize when his Muse was near, crediting his invisible Source for the content of the Jungle books, *Kim,* and both Puck books.

Madame Blavatsky, a Russian mystic who founded the Theosophical Society in 1875, claimed that the great Masters, who had knowledge of man's spiritual history, initiated her into the secrets of esoteric mysticism and helped her write the three-volume, 1,300-page *Secret Doctrine.* I found this

especially interesting and somewhat ironic. In the late 1980s and early 1990s, I was a member of a Theosophical study group in Wheaton, Illinois. We met on a regular basis and each member was encouraged to suggest a topic for further exploration by the group. Knowing Madame Blavatsky had used inspired writing to create *The Secret Doctrine,* I suggested we discuss the process of guided writing. My idea was immediately turned down. Although the description of the writing process for *The Secret Doctrine* is classic inspirational writing, it was a discouraged topic of discussion by the organization founded on that book's very principles.

In his book, *Channeling the Higher Self,* Henry Reed, PhD, relays the story of how author Richard Bach came up with the idea to write *Jonathan Livingston Seagull.* As the story goes, Bach was walking one day when he heard an inner voice repeat "Jonathan Livingston Seagull" over and over. "He went home and began writing immediately, furiously trying to keep up with the flow of words that were coming spontaneously to mind," wrote Reed. "In one sitting he provided the world with one of its most uplifting stories."

One of the most famous uses of "automatic" writing was by a St. Louis housewife named Pearl Curran. In the early 1900s, she worked with a spirit named Patience Worth, who had been a seventeenth-century English woman. Those messages turned into several thousand poems, a play, several novels, and many short pieces. Authorities have studied the writing of the alleged Patience Worth, and many have concluded that based on Curran's education and talent, she could not have written them on her own, especially since she used words that had disappeared from the English language long before her time.

William Stainton Moses was a well-educated, ordained minister in the Church of England during the mid-nineteenth century. He used guided writing to produce his books *Spirit Teachings* and *Spirit Identity*, saying he believed that the source of those writings came from higher spirits and were intended for good.

In writing his poem *Hyperion*, John Keats said that the description of Apollo was something that was given to him, as if another person wrote it.

In describing the writing of his novel *Werther*, German poet Goethe said he wrote it unconsciously, as if he were asleep, and added that he was amazed at the process.

English poet William Blake, in talking about his work *Milton*, said it felt as though he had written the poem from dictation without premeditation.

And then there's the remarkable story of Dr. Helen Schucman, who heard her inner voice say, "This is a course in miracles. Please take notes." In describing the process of writing *A Course in Miracles*, Schucman said that while she had grown accustomed to the unexpected, she still was very surprised when she wrote: "This is a Course in Miracles." This was her introduction to the "Voice," and, like Blake, Schucman described the process as a kind of rapid inner dictation.

Of all the famous writers who used a form of soul writing, the one I most identify with is Ruth Montgomery. A nationally syndicated news columnist, Montgomery admitted that many of her metaphysical books were created through what she called "automatic" writing. Each morning, she would sit at her desk in front of her typewriter, say a prayer, close her eyes, relax her fingers, and then her guide Lily and twelve others came through.

Arthur Ford, who by the mid 1950s was America's best-known living medium, introduced Montgomery to guided writing. She attended a talk he gave and afterward introduced herself as a reporter seeking an interview about the

Spiritual Frontier Fellowship, a new organization Ford was involved in that had been founded by educators, professionals, and clergy to investigate psychic phenomena.

After the interview, Ford offered to do a reading for Montgomery. He went into trance and his spirit control, Fletcher, came through. After Montgomery researched and then confirmed the information Fletcher provided, she wrote a two-page Sunday spread on Ford and his uncanny ability. Thereafter, the two became friends.

Several years passed before Ford suggested to Montgomery that she try automatic writing. He instructed her to attempt it for no more than fifteen minutes at a time and always at the same hour each day—the latter advice being similar to what Edgar Cayce had told writers nearly thirty years earlier.

Following Ford's suggestion, Montgomery sat at her desk at 8:30 every morning, said a prayer for protection, and entered a ten- to fifteen-minute meditation. During her trance, she picked up a pencil and held it over a piece of paper. For days nothing happened. Then one morning the pencil began to move in circles and figure eights. Several days later she began getting messages.

The turning point came when she found herself drawing a lily. The message she received informed her that this symbol was the identification of the source of her writing. From that day forward, Montgomery was greeted daily by the symbol of the flower and the word Lily. Afterward would flow what she called, "The most beautiful philosophy that I had ever read." Montgomery said she never had such inspiring thoughts.

Montgomery's initial writing sessions were done by hand, but when the sessions grew in strength and speed, her writing became illegible. She was instructed to "go to your typewriter," and thereafter got typewritten messages with little punctuation or capitalization. These sessions produced philosophical discourses that filled two to three pages each day.

Lily and the "Guides"—as Montgomery liked to call them—suggested she put their messages in books. At first she refused because she had too much going on in her life. An active member of the White House press corps, she faced a demanding schedule of writing columns, attending dinner parties, and a hectic traveling schedule that at that time included covering the 1960 Kennedy/Nixon presidential campaign.

When her frenzied lifestyle landed her in the hospital, she experienced the power of prayer. This gave her the desire to write a book, but one totally unrelated to her experiences. The book was not successful and her Guides quickly pointed out that this wasn't the type of book they had in mind. They gently suggested she not get involved with projects that wasted her time, but instead put her talents into producing material that would help others. Lily told Montgomery that she had no higher mission than to pass on to others the truths she was learning from the writing she had been receiving. And the rest, as they say, is history.

There is much to be said about writing in a dream state. That is, after all, a time when the unconscious mind is in control and can provide us with information that is not filtered by the more controlling waking consciousness. There certainly are a number of compositions that emanate from dreams to uphold that supposition. Robert Louis Stevenson, for instance, recorded his dreams and used them as the basis of his stories. He called his dream helpers his "brownies" and admitted to relying on them for help in the writing process.

With so many testimonials bearing witness to the existence of an unseen Source serving as a writer's Muse, it is easy to understand why, through the centuries, civilization

has accepted inspired writings as sacred messages. Spiritually illuminated works, such as the Bible, are not written *by* any one person, but are said to come *through* that person. The writer, therefore, becomes the vessel through which Spirit manifests its message. Certainly no one can argue the point that they contain wisdom far beyond the conscious awareness of those who put the words on paper.

These sacred writings—all written in an altered state of consciousness—have changed the course of history, yet today, as in past centuries, creative work accomplished by means of attuning to a higher power still is met with skepticism and, in some cases, scorn. Those who readily admit to employing this process are often labeled schizophrenic or mentally unstable. Nonetheless, messages obtained through the writer's profound connection to a Higher Source have transformed millions of lives. Each writer, understanding the process and sensing the connectedness to the All That Is, recognizes that his or her role is that of a messenger, conveying profound Truths in a way that can be digested by readers at all levels of awareness.

There is always some element of fear and stigma attached to writings that don't quite fit in society's conventional box. Nonetheless, throughout history, writers continually aspire to reach into that invisible realm and use their craft to attune to the Divine. Every writer yearns to form a sacred partnership with his or her Muse with the hope that it will produce powerful messages of transformation to benefit all mankind.

Frank DeMarco is one such writer. The co-founder of Hampton Roads Publishing Company and its chief editor for sixteen years, DeMarco helped to select and shape hundreds of books by authors known and unknown and soon-to-become known, including such luminaries as Richard Bach, Joseph McMoneagle, and Robert Bruce.

DeMarco is the author of two novels and three books of nonfiction, with more of each on the way. One of his books, *Chasing Smallwood,* is a record of conversations with a nineteenth-century American who provides a fascinating glimpse of life in the West and during the Civil War.

DeMarco consciously began learning to communicate with the other side in 1989. By then he had been keeping a journal for twenty-three years, and writing in this manner had become a comfortable habit. First he experimented with a form of automatic writing and then moved on to confident written dialogue.

"For the longest time, I would try to do automatic writing, and I would either get gibberish or I would get nothing," he told me. "I couldn't figure out how to put myself in a trance. I thought I was just a failure, but over time I evolved a method."

DeMarco credits The Monroe Institute (TMI) in Faber, Virginia, for deepening his connection to the other side. Founded by the late Robert Monroe, noted pioneer in the investigation of human consciousness and inventor of Hemi-Sync, TMI provides experiential six-day residential programs. In late 1992, DeMarco participated in TMI's Gateway Voyage program, which showed him how to get in closer touch with what he now calls "The Guys Upstairs." At this point, he was writing down the messages. Then early in 1993, at another TMI program, Guidelines, he first allowed others to come through in speech. This was followed by years of answering the questions posed by others while he held himself in an altered state.

"After the Guidelines program, it was a little of each—writing and speaking," he explained. "When I work with someone else, it is always oral. Working by myself, it is always written."

Even though he has a special relationship with The Guys Upstairs, DeMarco plays down the idea that individuals need to know the identity of their Source.

"It doesn't matter who's on the other end of the line, to a degree, because ultimately you're going to have information coming to you. You then have to judge whether it's valid or not; whether it resonates or not. What are you going to do? Are you going to get an affidavit saying what or who this really was?"

DeMarco's relationship with Spirit has evolved to the point where he sometimes does not know whether it's "himself" or "them" talking, but like knowing the identity behind the information, he doesn't think it makes much difference. "Half the time when I'm talking, I think it's them. They're sort of nudging me. When you say something that has a huge impact on somebody else and it just casually comes out of you, you're being used—but in a good way."

Reading *Chasing Smallwood,* you cannot help but wonder if Joseph Smallwood is actually a past-life aspect of Frank, which would mean that in essence, he was talking to himself. But DeMarco prefers not to discuss abstract questions like that.

"I wouldn't bother to describe the theory; I'd describe the process, because the theory could be all wrong. And even if the theory is right, it's not going to help you. The process was that I just sat down with my journal in the morning, and there he was."

DeMarco says he does not believe that he does automatic writing. In reviewing his technique, what he experiences certainly points in the direction of inspirational writing, especially since his handwriting does not change—one of the clear indications of inspired writing.

"The handwriting is no better than mine," he chuckled. "I have never seen a difference. When I tried it in 1989, I thought it would be different, and I actually tried to make it different, and I couldn't."

In fact, when writing with The Guys Upstairs, not only is DeMarco's handwriting the same, but so is the phrasing.

"They'll use my way of saying things. I sometimes know what's coming in, and I'll just write it as I know it. Sometimes they stop, and I can feel them searching for a way to say something. I'll suggest a word, and they'll quarrel with it."

An example of this happened during his communication with Joseph. DeMarco used the word "passport" and Joseph told him that the word was wrong. "It only occurred to me later that he had never heard of passports in the 1800s," said DeMarco. "He wanted to use the word 'warrant,' but I mildly quarreled with him over that because I did not know why I would use that particular word. Of course, the word 'warrant' doesn't mean the same thing to us as it does to someone in that time period."

If he were to describe his process to someone who had never done inspired writing before, DeMarco would say it's akin to writing a letter. You start the letter, and the rest of the words come as you keep writing.

"If I were to ask you: 'How did you do that?' you'd look at it closely, and you'd say you really don't know," he explained. "You have the intent to communicate. You know how you want to start and the words appear. Nonwriters find it hard to believe that what writers really do is make themselves accessible to 'it' and then wait to see what comes. A nonwriter thinks you must have known what you were going to write. What they don't realize is that they themselves don't know ahead of time what they're going to write. I can't say that I usually hear the words in my head, although that happens occasionally. The vast majority is just a knowing."

While famous writers, artists, and composers may not know exactly how their inspiration comes to them, each of them recognizes, in their own way, their role as the instrument through which this divinely inspired creativity flows.

CHAPTER TWO

My Early Experiences

As a young child, I displayed an endless fascination for anything having to do with the eighteenth century.

My particular area of interest was early American history. Books about Abigail Adams and Dolley Madison enthralled me. I loved watching movies with a historical backdrop; even though in those early days of television, they were few and far between.

When I was eight, I began taking classical piano lessons and efficiently played pieces by Bach, Beethoven, and Mozart in school concerts and competitions. Until I was thirteen and the Beatles came along, I preferred classical music to other genres and was especially fond of the harpsichord. My parents bought me a used piano, but I always had a secret longing to own a harpsichord—not exactly the kind of instrument you'd find in any of the homes in the blue-collar neighborhood where I grew up.

At Halloween I always tried to find a costume representing period clothing. My Aunt Rita, who lived next door, gave me all of her bridesmaids dresses, which in those days were designed to resemble fairytale ball gowns. Though not authentically eighteenth century, they were resplendent enough to satisfy my longing to live in a different time period.

When I grew older and visited novelty stores, I found quill pens that I began using to write by candlelight. Had I been more knowledgeable about reincarnation, I may have surmised that all of these fetishes were signs that I was drawing on an eighteenth-century past life, but I did not make that connection until years later.

Other than my channeling the Phoenician alphabet, I did not stumble into soul writing again until college, and then it emerged in an unexpected way. I was attending the University of Illinois, Chicago Circle. I had no particular career direction at that time. I enjoyed writing, but the Chicago campus was relatively new and did not offer a journalism department. I had developed an interest in reincarnation as a teenager and spent a lot of time wondering what it would have been like to live in different time periods. This fascination with the past led me to choose history as my major, although at this stage I did not connect the dots that my interest in reincarnation and my choice of history as a major had any similarities other than they both dealt with the past.

I admit I was a lazy student, preferring to daydream in the classroom and avoid the reading assignments. I may not have been diligent in my studies, but I did love to sit in on the lectures covering different aspects of early American life. A curious phenomenon occurred during these years. Despite my lack of scholastic discipline, during an essay exam my pen took on a life of its own, writing long missives in answer to the exam question. As the pen flew across the paper, at times I was not sure what I was writing. I may have entered the classroom with that panicked feeling every student gets

 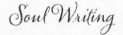

when they realize they are not prepared, but to my surprise, I almost always got an A on the exam.

This ability came to the forefront one summer when I enrolled in an American Constitution class. Our professor was the kind most students dread, belittling our academic skills whenever possible. He gave us an assignment: to research and write about a member of the Constitutional Convention. I chose an obscure delegate and happily spent hours in the library doing the research and putting the paper together. After reviewing our reports, our professor said that collectively he never read such bad work and insisted each of us must go to his office for a personal meeting.

I was prepared for the worst, but to my surprise he was highly complimentary of my work and gave me that coveted but seldom seen "A." After handing me the paper, he sat back and stared at me for what seemed an eternity until he finally spoke. "You know, you have the most *uncanny* feel for the eighteenth century of any student I've ever had." He encouraged me to continue doing historical research and to pursue a writing career.

I left his office, repeating his comment about my "uncanny feel" as a mantra. It was true. I knew what I was writing from a perspective that was totally foreign to me. It was simply a knowing. Luckily for me, whatever I was writing was exactly what he wanted to read.

Looking back, the only plausible explanation I can offer is that my memories of an eighteenth-century life, which are close to the surface in this lifetime, managed to break through to consciousness whenever I wrote about that time period. It would be another twenty years before I put two and two together and considered the possibility that I may have been in touch with the part of me that actually lived during that time period. How incredible to think I may not have been writing about events I had read about, but somehow may have been remembering what I had witnessed firsthand.

Again there was a lapse of many years before I pursued soul writing again. I began a career in advertising and used my writing skills to write brochures, ads, press releases, newsletters, and other promotional materials, and I later branched out into writing feature articles for newspapers and magazines. Naturally, this work was always done in a conscious state, and over the years, I developed a style that was uniquely my own.

Then in January 1987, Shirley MacLaine's *Out on a Limb* aired on ABC. Like thousands of other sleeping metaphysicians, it was a wake-up call for me to begin my esoteric journey. My friend Kelley decided we could start by exploring our past lives through her Ouija board. Like so many of the experiments I conducted in those early years, I had no idea that there was any danger in doing this. I would not find out until many years later that Ouija boards were listed as the number-two "no-no" by the A.R.E. for developing psychic abilities. We did, in fact, have problems with the Ouija board, and eventually it was thrown away by a psychic who slapped our hands and said, "Don't play with this again."

Before that happened, however, we used it nearly every night and connected with spirits who identified themselves as "John" (who worked through me) and "A. B." (who worked through Kelley). One evening, Kelley and her husband wanted to try the Ouija together, so I sat back while they played with the board. Since I had a hard time remembering the details of what we experienced during these sessions, I decided that I would sit with pen and paper in hand and record the letters as they came up. There were long pauses when nothing happened. During one such pause, my hand began moving, causing the pen to make ovals on the paper. I thought it odd but dismissed it as my body's impatient way of passing time. I watched this with minor amusement, thinking it must be unconscious doodling that came out of boredom. But when the ovals became letters and the letters became phrases, I started to pay attention.

I did not receive anything significant during my early attempts, but as I practiced each day, the phrases gradually lengthened to full sentences and finally into paragraphs. The writer identified himself as John Mellington. The content was elementary at best, but it had a style and tone unlike anything I had written before. I did not realize it at the time, but this was my introduction to "automatic" writing. I say "automatic" because this was a source coming from outside myself rather than from within.

Oblivious to the Pandora's box I was opening, I pursued this form of writing nightly. At first our correspondence was innocent enough, but then the nature of our relationship started to change when "John" began appearing in the guise of a small child to my son, Michael, who was three years old at the time. Michael began telling me that he saw a little boy hiding in the corner of our dining room. He said the little boy was a "ghost" and described him in such a way that I knew it was John. After that, mischievous things began happening. A bowl of Halloween candy toppled from the top of the refrigerator and a platter of lasagna flew across my kitchen counter. This psychic activity was not limited to my home. Over at Kelley's house, light bulbs were popping in nearly every room.

As Henry Reed writes, "Automatic writing does have its drawbacks. Cayce discourages using any dissociated automatisms, including the Ouija board, as a form of channeling. The major problem with them is that they form a channel of the subconscious mind. That means there's both good news and bad news."

My writing with John was my introduction to the bad news. By not taking the proper precautions, I had opened the door to lower-level spirits. Eventually John's poltergeist activities came to an end. I learned to use white light protection before I did any writing and then asked that only information for my "highest and best" would come forth. It was an important lesson to learn—one that I remember each time I begin a writing session. I shudder to consider the consequences had I not learned this lesson so early in my soul writing excursions.

CHAPTER THREE

Automatic versus Inspirational Writing

As I began to study soul writing and became more involved with my work in the A.R.E., I realized that my desire to write from a place of inspiration was the right intention but the wrong approach. Curious—and at the same time ignorant—about this newfound ability, I started to research the topic in greater depth and was surprised at the number of references to *automatic* writing. The more research I did, the more confused I became because, as discussed earlier, the term "automatic writing" often was interchanged with the phrase "inspirational writing" as if they were one and the same. I had encountered this mix-and-match terminology before, most notably with *hypnosis* and *guided imagery*. The latter is considered a more palatable phrase for mainstream audiences. I began looking into the various ways *automatic* writing and *inspirational* writing was described in contemporary literature.

Nearly every reference was to automatic writing rather than inspirational writing. Definitions were fairly consistent:

- ⊛ Writing that does not come from the conscious thoughts of the writer
- ⊛ A channeling technique allowing your higher self or another entity to use your hands to write a message
- ⊛ Writing without using the conscious mind
- ⊛ Writing in a trance state

Differentiating between inspirational and automatic writing can lead to more questions than answers. For instance, if the inspiration is coming from a loving spirit guide or an angelic source, or if one believes it is coming from the Creator, then technically the information is coming from outside oneself and would be considered *automatic* writing. However, it can be argued that information from highly evolved spirit guides, angels, and certainly from the Creator qualify as coming from a "Higher Source" through the writer, and therefore fit the criteria of *inspirational* writing.

To understand the difference between the two, we need look no further than the Cayce readings. Writers came to Edgar Cayce asking how to improve their writing. Often they referred to doing automatic writing. Cayce made it clear that there was a difference between automatic writing and inspirational writing and said that the difference was in its purpose. When asked what could be gained from doing inspirational writing, Cayce suggested writing, "of things pertaining to mental and spiritual aspects of individuals grasping for attunement to the divine" (3653-1). He also said inspirational writing is a way of getting to the truth. "To know the truth is to make you free! Truth is as Life, a GROWING consciousness in self" (323-2).

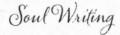

(The Cayce readings are numbered to maintain confidentiality. The first number [e.g., 3653] refers to the individual or group for whom the reading was given. The second number refers to which reading it was [i.e., first, second, third, etc.].)

Cayce considered inspirational writing as coming from the Source within, and, as such, it is a means for soul development. Automatic writing, on the other hand, came from an outside source, which is sometimes comprised of low influences (like my little poltergeist John). Cayce warned that there were seekers (spirits) on the outside who were always looking for a way to communicate and that their influence is not always for one's highest and best. He advised that only God should direct those attempting to do inspirational writing. Advice that is directing, guiding, impelling, or advising to turn against God is coming from the wrong folks.

In his book *Venture Inward,* Hugh Lynn Cayce (Edgar Cayce's son), shared case histories of individuals who experienced the detrimental effects of automatic writing. In one case, he told of a woman who, in describing her experience with automatic writing, claimed: "They use my hand and control my nervous system in such a way that they write through me, and my brain does not anticipate what will be written." She said at first she received messages from departed family members, as well as instructions on what she needed to do to prepare for the work ahead. She later claimed that the late Edgar Cayce came through and communicated to her that he was the source of the writing.

About a month later, however, her tone changed. "The devil, that vile wretch," she wrote in a letter to Hugh Lynn. "He wanted to pass himself off last night but I would not trust him because I know him after five days of harassing by him."

Things seemed to go downhill from there as she described

"an overpowering obsession by what must have been thousands of disembodied spirits. What I've gone through nobody else, I hope, will ever know. I was a novice and nobody warned me, except you. . . . For several weeks I was under their control to the extent I could not move, lift an eyelash, or even speak without their allowing it."

Cases like these involving spirit obsession are why Edgar Cayce went to such lengths to describe the difference between the two types of writing—to warn of the dangers of one but encourage the exploration of the other.

"Cayce notes that writing automatically, with the subconscious mind as the source of the material, results primarily simply in the production of channeled material," Henry Reed wrote. "What comes through may affect the person (hopefully not in a detrimental way), but there's no growth in the process itself. It's more like learning a trick than learning to grow in consciousness." Therefore, Reed concludes that inspirational writing is more valuable than automatic writing "because it helps you grow in your awareness."

Even though Cayce did not encourage it, what is fascinating in the readings is the advice he gave to those asking how they could do *automatic* writing. As we can see in the following readings, Cayce admonished some not to attempt it at all, while others he not only encouraged but also gave detailed instructions on how to proceed. When asked if the development of automatic writing would establish a better contact with God, Cayce answered, "For this body we would not give automatic writing as the channel. Rather the intuitional, or the meditation and then writing – KNOWING what is being written, if it's chosen to be inscribed in ink" (440-8).

Another inquired, "You told me that anyone could do automatic writing. Will you please tell me how I may develop it?" Cayce answered, "By practice. Sit alone with pencil and paper, and let that guide that may be sought – or may come in – direct. It will come" (262-25).

On the surface, this advice may seem contradictory. Why raise a red flag about the dangers of automatic writing to one and then give the green light to proceed to another? The dual advice stemmed from Cayce's ability to read a person's intent and temperament. While Cayce believed it is everyone's birthright to communicate with Source, he was nonetheless adamant that preparation was essential before proceeding. Those who are engaged in prayer and meditation, who have an ideal and know their purpose, are more suited to the practice than those who have not worked on their spiritual development to any degree before.

"Cayce's formula for developing the channel of inspirational writing is similar to our general formula for channeling," wrote Henry Reed. "First we tune ourselves to our ideal, and then we step aside to allow spontaneous expression."

While it may appear that Cayce condoned automatic writing for some and not others, one thing is for certain. He consistently drove home the message that inspirational writing was the preferred method of communication with Spirit.

> Do not attempt to write as one who would do automatic writing. Do attempt to write as one who would be directed by inspiration, but let that inspiration come from Him, who is light, and the source of knowledge; and thus may the individual in its choice and in its activities be so surrounded by the Christ-consciousness, manifested by and through Jesus of Nazareth, that there will be ever helpful forces (5277-1).

After studying the Cayce readings on automatic and inspirational writing, Henry Reed broke down the major differences between the two:

AUTOMATIC	INSPIRATIONAL
No awareness of writing	Awareness of what's being written
No control of hand movements	Allow writing to proceed on its own
Handwriting happens by itself	Consciously watch thoughts reveal themselves through subconscious
Handwriting different	Handwriting same

Over the years, I have developed a method that is a hybrid of the two. I am aware of what's being written the moment it appears on paper, but not necessarily before then—that is, I have no preconceived notion of what will appear on paper until one or two words ahead of time. I put little pressure on the pen but can feel a difference in my arm and hand during the process. While I can stop writing at any time, I allow the writing to proceed unimpeded until the message is complete. The biggest difference in my process is that my penmanship is different from the way I write in a conscious state.

My method does not fit the accepted definition of either automatic or inspirational writing, but that could be because there has been a genre shift in the definition of inspirational writing since Cayce wrote about it in the 1930s and 1940s. Browse the titles on Amazon.com under "Inspirational Writing" and you will find most are tied to the Christian writing genre, while the top "Automatic Writing" titles are solidly in the occult category. But *neither* contains books that describe inspirational writing the way Cayce intended. This is one of the reasons why I prefer to use the term "Soul Writing," as I feel it is a better term to capture the spirit of what Mr. Cayce meant by inspirational writing. Guided writing, meditative writing, revelation writing, visionary writing, or even visceral writing are other possible terms, but, frankly, none of them seem right. It appears that the English language is limited in producing a word that encompasses all of the elements of this remarkable tool of transformation.

CHAPTER FOUR

How to Establish a Writing Ritual

Anyone can learn how to do soul writing. Most get something on their first try. With practice, nearly everyone succeeds. Based on the advice given by Edgar Cayce, and from my own experience, I have come up with a twelve-step program to gain optimal results when starting a soul writing session.

(1) Find a Sacred Place

If you come to Charlottesville, Virginia, and tour Monticello, the home of Thomas Jefferson, you'll pass through his private suite, which one of his guests referred to as his "sanctum sanctorum." Few people were allowed access to these rooms during his lifetime. This is where he read and sat with his Muse while expressing his genius on paper.

Everyone needs a "sanctum sanctorum." While it is true

that you can write anywhere, you can create your own sacred writing space with the aesthetic qualities most conducive to your connection to Spirit.

Some people are more sensitive to energies than others, but nearly everyone has an intuitive knowing of when someone, someplace, or something isn't quite right. For instance, have you ever walked into a space and felt uncomfortable there, wanting nothing more than to leave as quickly as possible? On the flip side, have you ever gone somewhere new and felt your soul take a collective sigh, as if you happily could remain there forever? I often have done this, "feeling" out the places I resonate to on that deepest level. When I find a space where I feel surrounded by loving energies, the first words out of my mouth usually are—"I really can see myself writing here."

Houses—like people—are made up of energetic vibrations, making certain rooms more conducive to spiritual work than others. Find the place in your home that speaks to you and then establish that as the sacred place where you will connect with Spirit. Quiet, privacy, soft lighting, and a comfortable place to sit are the primary requirements. The ideal space may be your bedroom, the guest room, your office, your kitchen, the basement, or a corner of your living room. During my soul writing research project, my volunteer participants said their bedroom was the most popular place to write, although one connected to Spirit in her family room and another wrote at the kitchen table.

I have written in three places in my home—in my bedroom, in my lower-level office, and on my front porch. The last I can only do when conditions are right—when the weather is accommodating, and my neighborhood is quiet enough that I can sit undisturbed. I have experienced many profound writing sessions from my front porch, including an entire session on Universal Laws versus the Ten Commandments (see chapter 8).

I always take my journal and my favorite pen with me when I travel. I have written everywhere: a hotel balcony overlooking the ocean, on a screened-in porch surrounded by an Arizona desert landscape, or at the kitchen table of a rented condo in the mountains at Wintergreen, Virginia. That's the beauty of soul writing. Your ability to connect with Spirit is always with you, no matter where you are. It is, by far, one of the most comforting elements of this work.

While it is true that you can write anywhere, as a beginner you may find that locating that special place in your own home is well worth the investment. When looking for the "ideal" space for you to connect with Spirit, feel out the energy of the space you are in. Sense where you feel peaceful and centered, then claim that space for your own.

(2) Set the Stage

Now that you have the right space, surround yourself with items that enable you to go into a deeper state of meditation. In reading 3653-1, Cayce said, "Here is one entity who may write, not automatic but rather inspirational writing, shutting itself away and attuning itself by very distant music, and especially bells."

When I was doing deep soul writing to connect to my eighteenth-century lifetime, I created an atmosphere that was conducive to that time period. I played soft classical music in the background, turned off everything that relied on electricity, lit enough candles to see by, took out my journal and fountain pen, and off I went. It worked every time.

I mentioned that I have written in numerous places while traveling. These places may have one or two elements that are conducive to my writing, but because I am traveling, I do not always have my consciousness-raising items around me. When I am home in my sacred space, I am surrounded by artwork, candles, crystals, and spiritual books that have a particular meaning to me. You may find that items that have a special place in your soul—things that remind you of your spiritual journey—may help to deepen your connection with Spirit when doing soul writing. Whether it is a dream catcher, totem, plants, or photographs, find those things that resonate with you on a deep soul level and sit with them for a while. Feel their energy. Remember their meaning to you. Let them lift you higher as you communicate with Source.

As Cayce suggested, you also can attune your inner self through music or bells. At an A.R.E. conference I attended a few years ago, author Julia Cameron introduced the audience to music from *The Yearning: Romances for Alto Flute,* by Michael Hoppé and Tim Wheater. The vibration of the flute resonated with me on a deep level. While everyone was quietly breathing in these luscious tones, tears were cascading down my cheeks. I knew I had just been introduced to music that would take my writing deeper. I bought the CD and have used it in my meditations ever since.

Think about the music that you resonate to—the music that brings meaningful visualizations into your mind's eye; the music that you absorb with eyes closed that takes you deeper and deeper into a relaxed state. This is the music of your soul and it—as with other treasures you use to set the stage—is a key element in your spiritual writing session.

(3) Same Time, Same Place

With our busy schedules, it may be difficult to connect with Spirit at the same time and place each day, but Cayce suggests doing just that for optimal results.

 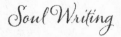

First, under the circumstances and conditions that surround the body, it would be well that an hour or period
be chosen for such activities when there is quiet, and
when the mental and material body may become per-
fectly relaxed . . . And such periods should be chosen
as an exact period. Say (as an illustration), 10:00 to
10:30 o'clock in the evening, the period is chosen . . .
Enter then in this silence, each evening, at this specific
time (282-5).

Many people prefer to write first thing in the morning,
before their mind becomes preoccupied with events of the
day. In her book *The Artist's Way,* author Julia Cameron talks
about the value of finding inspiration and clarity in what she
calls Morning Pages. She suggests writing a stream of consciousness by hand—enough to produce three pages of whatever comes to mind. While this may not fit the criteria of soul
writing, her suggestion to write the first thing in the morning
certainly can apply to soul writing. Doing so will set the tone
for the day and give you a greater awareness of what to look
for over the next twenty-four hours.

It seems as though it is in the wee hours of the morning
when our world is most quiet that it is easier to hear divine
guidance. Awakening at 3:00 a.m. is a nightly occurrence
for many soul writers. Since time only exists on our plane of
existence, if the Creative Forces have something to convey
to you, they will do whatever it takes to get your attention,
even if that means rousing you from a deep sleep. If you wake
up at that early hour and have enough energy to pick up
your pen and journal, you may be surprised at what comes
through.

Obviously not everyone is a morning person. Many prefer to write at night, just before going to sleep, thus putting
themselves—and the events of the day—to bed. I have found

that getting into an altered state right before bed is a wonderful way to shake off the cares of the day, to relinquish stress, and slip into a state of deep relaxation. Instead of writing about what is ahead, as I do in the morning, my nighttime writings review the events of the day. Like an unfolding scroll, it presents everything I experienced and gives me the luxury of time to think about issues that were presented to me, how I handled them, and what lessons they contained.

Writing at night puts the period after the last sentence of my day's script and says—okay, that's done. Now let's get some sleep and prepare for tomorrow's lessons. There is, however, one downside to night writing. If you are someone who can be lulled to sleep easily, this is a sure-fire way to drift off to dreamland before a single word appears on paper!

Whether it's first thing in the morning, midday, or before bed, one of the most compelling reasons to write at the same time each day is that it establishes a pattern. Humans are creatures of habit. Getting into the rhythm of consistently writing every day at a specific time becomes a natural part of our routine. Nevertheless, if this isn't already a part of your daily agenda, creating a new writing pattern presents challenges of its own. It requires a willingness to change and to put forth a consistent effort day after day. If you can make that commitment and stick to it, you will find that creating a daily writing pattern is a proven way to achieve success.

At the risk of saying, "Do as I say and not as I do," I admit I no longer write at a consistent time. When I was a novice at soul writing, I wrote every evening before going to bed. However, as the years passed and my schedule changed, I stopped writing at a specific time. Today if I am in need of guidance, I stop what I am doing, get comfortable, do a brief meditation, say a prayer of protection, and seek the answer to whatever question or issue is before me.

Communication is a two-way process. After years of practice, I have come to recognize when my higher self has something to say. In a manner of speaking, I feel as though someone is ringing my soul's doorbell. I tell my friends "I'm getting buzzed." That usually brings about some snickering. I think of it in the context of the sound of a doorbell in the lobby of an apartment complex. Spirit is leaning on my doorbell, asking to come in and chat a while, or I'm leaning on some unseen etheric doorbell, asking for entrance into the spiritual realm. Luckily, Spirit is *always* home, *always* at the end of the line, *always* waiting for your call. Regardless of when you decide to check in, setting aside time each day to connect with Spirit is a date you won't want to break.

(4) Pen versus Keyboard

Writing with a pencil, a pen, or on a keyboard is a matter of personal preference. Many famous writers are able to access Spirit at a keyboard. Julia Cameron told an A.R.E. audience that she has a prayer on her computer that asks God to take care of the quality while she takes care of the quantity. Many other writers, like Ruth Montgomery, composed on a keyboard with positive results.

I have done both, but as I indicated earlier, I prefer to write by hand using a fountain pen. My entire past-life manuscript was done in this manner. Interestingly, when working on that project I occasionally looked for a faster way of writing, so I put the pen and journal down, got up and went to my computer. I placed my fingers gently on the keyboard, waiting for the next sentence to appear. Nothing came. I tried again, saying my prayer of protection, encouraging my higher self to continue our session and still nothing. The moment I turned off the computer and picked up my fountain pen and journal, the writing returned. Different strokes for different folks!

Certainly you are as guided at the computer as you are with pen in hand. However, it takes more time and patience to write by hand. It also has a different feel to it than composing on a keyboard. When writing by hand, you sense a spiritual presence is within, gently guiding your hand. You know what is being written, but you don't have to stop and think about it. When you sit at a computer and poise your hands over a keyboard, some part of you must remain in a conscious state in order to remember the location of the appropriate keys. One key off, and you won't be able to read the message. Having to consistently check the placement of your fingers on the keyboard can disrupt the flow of the message because it pulls you in and out of an altered state of consciousness.

As a professional writer, I can tell the difference between the style and quality of the writing I do by hand versus what I write on a keyboard. Whenever I am working on a feature article or a public relations or a marketing campaign for a client—I do it on the computer. When I take off my professional writing hat and find a quiet place in which to meditate, and with pen in hand check in with myself to see what's happening on a deeper level, then the writing is completely different in tone and style. This is because the source of inspirational writing is a higher state of consciousness.

It is hard for young people to imagine, but it wasn't too long ago that there were no keyboards. Our historical inspired writing all comes from the handwritten word. It does not matter that the revelations of those great books were written thousands of years ago, for time does not exist for the Creative Forces. The writers of those holy books had access to the same source that we do. Same source. Same information. Same result. But all written in a way that is a unique expression of our individuality. Everyone who transcribes their guidance on paper does so with a different feel, a different message, a different sound—and a different cadence. It is the latter—the rhythm of the message—that is especially apparent when writing by hand.

Something transformative happens when I write by hand versus on the keyboard. In her article "The Value of Writing by Hand," author Heather Sellers described the difference in the sensation that handwriting elicits, saying it was truer, fresher, stranger, and purer. The words came from "some place where the heart meets the soul in the land of the unconscious—the same place DREAMS come from."

Writing by hand definitely slows you down. It gives your brain a chance to work with your body in a kind of spiritual union from which your best work will emerge. To find out which method is best for you, experiment with the keyboard and the pen or pencil. Start by selecting your favorite writing instrument. You don't have to spend a fortune by investing in a rare or expensive fountain pen (although who wouldn't revel at writing with one!). It could be a ballpoint that glides easily across the page, or it could be a mechanical pencil with an ever-sharp point. Scribble with different pens and pencils until you find the right one for you and then write with it over a period of a few days. Then switch to the keyboard to record your messages electronically over a similar length of time. Afterward, decide which method of writing you prefer and commit to that.

If you decide to write by hand, you will need to find the right kind of paper. Many writers use a lined legal pad. Others prefer to write on loose-leaf paper they can put in a three-ring binder. Still others—like myself—prefer journals. When I first started, I used an unlined, saddle-stitched five-by-seven-inch journal with a pretty floral cover. Now I prefer larger 8½ x 11–inch, lined, spiral-bound journals whose pages lie flat. That makes it easy to turn the pages completely around so that I can write efficiently on one page at a time.

It does not matter what you write with or what you write on. What matters is that you write—period!

(5) Focus on an Ideal

Cayce says one must be true to one's convictions. When asked in a reading what could be done to raise the quality of the seeker's writing, Cayce replied:

> There is self, there is the force without thee. What seekest thou? Art thou opening thyself to any, or art thou one that has set a standard, an ideal? Like begs like, whether in the mental, spiritual or physical realm. What seekest thou? Answer that in self, and we may find that as ye seek ye may know. This is to every soul: Once to every soul is given the knowledge that thou hast a definite purpose to perform in everything that has come under thine own consciousness. What has thou done about it? (317-7)

In *A Search for God,* an ideal is defined as something beyond and above us toward which we build. The true ideal "is the highest spiritual attainment to be reached on this material plane." Everything in our life is measured against it—and everyone, whether they realize it or not, works with an ideal on some level of their consciousness. It's a guiding pattern in your life—the "why" of why you do the things you do and say the things you say. The ideal is often something missing in your life and in your relationship to others. Perhaps you are working on tolerance, forgiveness, patience, or compassion. Cayce said knowing and working with your ideal is one of the most important experiences of every soul who incarnates.

You can define your ideal in a single word, a phrase, or an entire sentence. Henry Reed said that he found that meditating on his ideal creates a "resonance with the creative energies patterned by the ideal" and "often provides an immediate channel of inspiration." Reed says to be a constructive channel for inspirational writing, we need to attune to an ideal. "We allow our whole being, mind and body, to resonate with the spiritual energy of the ideal. Then when we let our thoughts flow directly onto paper they will reflect and express that spirit. Here we have inspired writing, a channel of the higher self." He adds: "The ideal serves as both a magnet and a filter for what will pass through the channel."

What are some of the ways individuals have expressed their spiritual ideal? Often it is the expression of a person's mission in life; that is, to be a catalyst for change, to be a truth seeker, to attract prosperity, and to manifest love.

Cayce (1998-1) says, "First, know thy ideal, - spiritually, mentally, materially. Not so much as to what you would like others to be, but what may be YOUR ideal relationships to others! For he that is the greatest is the servant of all - as the law of cause and effect."

Before you begin your writing session, formulate your ideal in your mind, write it down, focus on it, and repeat it as a silent mantra. Then step aside and allow the response to flow.

(6) Meditation Is Key

Soul writing is a written form of meditation, and you cannot meditate if you are distracted. Rest assured, distraction will happen on multiple levels. Not only will you experience distractions on a physical level through sights and sounds, but you will also encounter distractions on the emotional and mental side because you will think too much about the process and stop the flow.

You'll question the source. You'll grow impatient and think about a conversation you had earlier. You'll want to control what's being written.

Cayce was asked, "Should body-mind attempt to develop powers for automatic writing as a means for expressing either his intuition or messages from guiding spirits or the universal forces?" In his response, Cayce talked about the importance of finding a quiet time to write with Spirit.

> First, under the circumstances and conditions that sur-
> round the body, it would be well that an hour or period
> be chosen for such activities when there is quiet, and
> when the mental and material body may become per-
> fectly relaxed (282-5).

Henry Reed wrote, "Meditation, in fact, is what Cayce prescribes as the first step in beginning a session of inspirational writing. We meditate to attune our consciousness to our ideal, to the highest within us. At the end of the meditation, we simply continue our attunement by expressing it in writing."

Reed goes on to say, "Inspirational writing is really an extension of meditation, so all of Cayce's advice on preparing for meditation applies here as well." Deep breathing is part of the process that enables you to attain a more profound level of meditation. He adds, "In meditative breathing, we are aware of the breathing process. Like automatic breathing, the flow of the breath happens by itself."

(7) Say a Prayer of Protection

Saying a prayer and asking for protection before working with Spirit is an imperative part of the process, and everyone should do it—whether you're an established psychic or a novice at metaphysical work. Every one of us has a special frequency, and we tune into Spirit on that frequency. If the channel is open, we will receive guidance that is pure, clear, and easily understood. There will be no static, no straining to hear the message, wondering if we got it right.

Sometimes—whether because of illness, depression, anger, alcohol, drugs, or other issues—our frequency is lowered. That's when you must be cautious, for that is when you enable less highly evolved energies to penetrate that little crack in your aura and interfere with your communiqués. Just as positive energy brings guidance for your highest good, lesser energies can run interference when there is something they don't want you to know. Don't give them an open-door invitation. Asking for white light protection ensures that you are sealed in an impenetrable bubble, strengthens your aura, and wards off any dark energy that might be looking for an opening. You may think you are immune to the danger of these lower energies, but even the most experienced, spiritually aware individuals can blindly stumble into the overconfidence trap.

I attended a conference once where the speaker—whose claim to fame was his ability to "channel" angels—told the audience that saying a prayer of protection was not necessary and admitted that he never surrounded himself with white light protection before beginning a channeling session. He shared a story about a client who was contemplating suicide and wanted to ask his guardian angel if it would be all right for him to end his life. The channeler hesitated but finally said that the man's guardian angel had made it clear that suicide was an acceptable option. Two weeks later, the man took his life, leaving a wife and two small children behind. At the risk of sounding judgmental, what "angel" would give that kind of advice? The fact that this channeler did not believe in the need for white light protection may have resulted in lower energies coming in and, masquerading as an angel, been responsible for that devastating advice.

Prayer is an important step that should never be omitted. When I first began doing guided writing, I got a little cocky. I had no patience for ritual. I wanted to jump in and get my message so I could go on with whatever else I was doing. On two occasions I skipped saying a prayer of protection, and on both occasions I got into trouble. I could feel the energy shift in my arm and into my hand. It did not feel right and was unlike anything I had experienced before. The writing came out in tiny letters, nearly impossible to read, and the words went up diagonally on the page rather than in the usual horizontal manner. After this—as with my use of the Ouija board—there was an increase in poltergeist activity in my home, and I had to enlist the aid of a psychic to free me of that dark energy.

Cayce strongly urges saying a prayer or affirmation to magnify the presence of constructive influences.

> Then, enter in the silence with some form of rote that is rather in the form of a prayer, or as an affirmation to the inner self, that the forces or powers that may manifest through self at such a period may ever magnify the presence of not only constructive influence, but from the throne of grace and mercy itself (282-5).

In reading 849-76, Cayce was asked for a prayer that could be used while writing. He responded with the following:

FATHER-MOTHER-GOD! IN THY MERCY, IN THY LOVE, BE THOU THE GUIDE JUST NOW, AS I SEEK IN HUMILITY AND IN EARNESTNESS TO PRESENT THAT WHICH MAY GIVE MY FELLOW MAN A BETTER AND A MORE PERFECT INSIGHT INTO THE

 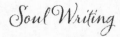

LOVE WHICH WAS MANIFESTED BY JESUS, MY
LORD AND MY GOD. HELP, THOU, O GOD, MY
EVERY EFFORT.

I say my own prayer of protection to discourage any low
influences from entering the bubble of white light I put
around myself when I write. You can make up a prayer of
your own, or if you're more comfortable, use a version of
the "Prayer of Protection" by the late James Dillet Freeman,
Unity's Poet Laureate:

> *The light of God surrounds you,*
> *The love of God enfolds you,*
> *The power of God protects you,*
> *The presence of God watches over you;*
> *Wherever you are, God is.*

Needless to say, I never skip saying a prayer, and I caution
you to do the same. Always ask for the highest good and that
no harm come to all—and so it will be.

(8) Get Ready to Write

To help get you started, Cayce said, "Sit with a subdued
or shaded light, with paper, pencil, or materials before self
at a desk or table" (282-5). Some writers visualize themselves
sitting in front of a peaceful lake or walking through a forest.
As they do, words come into their head, and they start writing
them down.

Patience and trusting your Source are essential, because
inspirational writing is a spontaneous process. For it to suc-
ceed, you have to get out of the way. If you try to manipulate
or force the words, you will disrupt the process.

Write (or, in your mind, state) the intent for the session. With soul writing, as in prayer, keep in mind the adage of "ask and you shall receive." If you want guidance regarding a specific issue, present the question in a very precise clear manner; for example, "Can you help me understand the underlying issue that is causing the disharmony between me and my sister?" Ask questions about what's bothering you. The deeper the question, the deeper the reply.

Put the date on the page. This is invaluable, especially when you review the messages years down the road. Open your eyes halfway so you can see the paper or screen in front of you. Keep your wrist(s) loose. Hold the pen or pencil loosely in your hand. If you are working on a keyboard, poise your fingers above the keys and wait.

(9) Allow the Message to Proceed

Getting started is always the most difficult part of the process. Impatience sets in, and we give up. It is important to be patient while simultaneously keeping the writing process going. Keep the wrist loose and just start with writing ovals. Eventually the words will follow. Each time you sit down for a session of soul writing, the first words will take the longest. You'll also find that your most inspired writing won't be these first words, even though you may have spent five minutes selecting them. Your best work will appear while you're writing, and it will be material you didn't have even a second to think about first.

It is true that the meat of the message usually comes somewhere in the middle. You may start out receiving ordinary, everyday guidance, then it gradually becomes more profound. There have been sessions in which I start writing and wonder where the message is going. If I persist, I am usually rewarded with something profound that comes midpoint, then the winding down that reinforces the message and provides the encouragement to follow through.

Some people get a specific greeting and farewell during their session. This generally happens when you have been working with the same Source for a while and there is a familiarity between you.

For the last twenty years, I have been greeted by one of two salutations: *"My dear child, we are with you always in love and in light"* or *"My dear child, you are in the light of God so fear nothing."* The farewell statement is usually a variation of *"We leave you in love and light."*

As the message appears, it is not uncommon for it to be short and to the point. Most messages are only a few paragraphs long. Cayce suggested to one writer, "Be not too long or too loud in thy words" (2800-2).

Everyone receives messages in a different way. Some people get a few phrases. Others get paragraphs. The sentences I receive generally are no more than a page of copy at any given time, but I also have experienced messages going on for multiple pages.

Those new to the process may only get a few scribbles on the page. It is important not to get discouraged, but just go with the flow. When I have given classes on soul writing, those who failed to get a message the first time around admitted they were afraid to let go and get out of the way. They wanted to be in control. Despite my warnings to allow the message to proceed on its own and to get out of their heads, they weren't able to completely relax and trust Spirit to provide the very guidance they so desperately wanted.

The words will come in their own time. They also will stop in their own time. It is an instinctual process that is different for everyone. You will know when it is time to start writing, just as you will know when the message is complete. No one can tell you when that happens. As with every aspect of soul writing, it is really a matter of trust.

With inspirational writing, it is important to write it as it comes. Transcribe the first thought that enters your mind. If possible, write fast. Do not let your internal editor complain about how the writing looks, how a word is spelled, or that the punctuation or grammar is incorrect.

Deep soul writing is between you and your Source. It is not designed to be critical or bully you into a change of attitude. It is never negative. It does not tell you what to do, but instead gently offers guidance on options to consider. It does not challenge you. It does not use foul language. If you get that, you need to stop immediately. Go back, say the prayer of protection again and reinforce your white light protection. Remember that soul writing comes from a very high level. Your loving Source would never call you names or make demands.

Write down whatever you receive. Don't begin to question it (unless it absolutely does not feel right), and don't shut down and refuse to hear the message. Remain open and receptive. Remember, you are asking for divine guidance. You may not always like what you hear, but if you proceed with an open heart, you will embrace the results.

Sometimes you may receive the same message over and over again. When I first started writing, I only received three words—"You are _____" (my past-life name, let's say Jane); so I got "You are Jane," "You are Jane," "You are Jane," over and over. It wasn't until I accepted the message that it stopped and then the guidance continued.

You will find that most soul writing includes the word "We" rather than "I." For instance, consider my greeting— "We are with you always" or "We leave you in love and light." The use of the word "we" lifts you higher into the collective

Soul Writing

consciousness. It reinforces a sense that you are never alone; that you are part of the collective Universe, in balance and harmony with the All That Is. When you write, you can refer to "I," but don't be surprised when your answer comes back in plural form, even though you may think of your higher self, angel, or Source as singular.

With soul writing, you do not know in advance what is going to appear on the paper by more than a word or two. As stated before, one of the sure ways to stop the process is to think about it too much or to read the message and try and comprehend it while it is still unfolding. Do not worry about sentence structure. Often the sentences will run on and on, without benefit of periods. There are times when I am writing and the words are all strewn together, and when I get to the end of the line, my pen slides across the paper to the left-hand column and I continue writing. It is akin to typing on an old typewriter where you pull the carriage back to the left when you come to the end of the paper. I half expect to hear a "ding" when I get to the end of the line!

(10) Wait before You Read

Writing is like a fine wine. It is best when it ages. Resist the temptation to go back and reread what you wrote immediately after the session ends. Words that sit for a while mysteriously transform from the mundane to the profound. Often when you put the writing away and go back to it a few days, weeks, or months later, it has a totally new meaning. The words awaken you to new possibilities and metaphysical concepts you had not considered before, and you will ask yourself, "Did I really write this?"

Cayce discussed the benefit of setting aside messages received through inspirational writing for another day.

What is given, or that [which] as an impelling influence causes to write, WRITE; and do not re-read, but put away for at least the period until it is given from within to review or to go over that which has been given . . . Do not grow weary if in turns with self nothing comes for perhaps days, or that much is given at one period in the beginning and little or nothing later. Be true to self, not to read nor HAVE read that written—until it is GIVEN thee to do so (282-5).

When you do read the message, do so from your spiritual self. Take a moment to reflect on the message and see if it resonates with you on any level. Does it expand your wisdom? Does it add to your knowledge? Does it amplify your truth? Does it awaken something deep within? Does it contain that spiritual "aha" moment? Has Spirit filled in the blanks and given you a deeper understanding of what's really going on in your life?

Guidance from your higher self is not intended to be a roadmap to tell you which way to go. Instead its purpose is to offer you a new perspective so that you can begin to see things differently. Ask yourself if the writing has done that for you. I know from my experience that this often happens. I find myself saying, "I never thought of that." This is when I am most grateful to have this indispensable tool at my disposal. I read the message with eyes, heart, and soul wide open and always, always express my gratitude with two simple words—thank you.

(11) Keep Your Writing Safe

Just as it is important to wait before you read, it is equally important to safeguard your writings from prying eyes. If ever there was a Pandora's box, this is it. Most of the time, the information you receive when doing soul writing is intended for your eyes only. Remember, deep soul writing is a conversation with your higher self, your guides, your Source, or your angel—with emphasis on the word *your.* When you are writing, you may be working out issues regarding relationships with friends and family members. You may be admitting to having done or thought things that you don't necessarily want others to know.

As we will explore later, deep soul writing is often used for psychoanalysis. It's like reclining on a chaise in a therapist's office and pouring out your soul, expressing your frustrations, your desires, your hopes and fears. When you tap into divine guidance through channeled writing, issues will be brought up that may trigger an unexpected emotional response. While you are working out the source of that emotion with your higher self, do you really want your best friend, your parent, your child, or your spouse to be eavesdropping on such an intimate conversation?

This is especially important for professional writers who use soul writing to explore different ideas and scenarios. You may be working out issues that happened in a past life, but to the casual reader, it appears you are writing about yourself in the here and now. Your "what ifs" may be your way of exploring various options about that life, but the reader may think you are recording an actual event in this life. You can imagine where this could lead.

I know this from firsthand experience. One day I came home unexpectedly and saw copies of my journal pages strewn across the kitchen table. In an instant, I knew that a family member had gone through my things, pulled out the journals, and not only read them, but was in the process of making copies of specific pages. Demanding an explanation, I was told this was done to "get to know me better." This breach of trust caused irreparable damage that continues to have ramifications to this day—all because of curiosity on their part and naïveté on mine.

Take my advice. Do not share your personal writings with anyone. If you insist on keeping your musings, then at the very least put them in a locked cabinet. If what you've written is a generic message that has some value to mankind, then by all means share it, but if it contains anything of a personal nature, do what you can to protect it from prying eyes.

(12) A Few Final Dos and Don'ts

Concluding my advice about how to establish a writing ritual, I'd like to offer a few other tidbits to make the experience that much more successful and worthwhile.

- Inspirational writing is a tool of transformation. Be prepared for your life to change once you begin writing on a regular basis.

- If you are going through an especially difficult time, writing can be a powerful tool on the road to recovery. However, if you are experiencing emotional or mental health issues, seek counseling first, then use inspired writing as an adjunct to that therapy.

- Do not try soul writing when you are under the influence of anything like drugs, tobacco, alcohol, junk food, etc., that may cause your system to slow down or speed up. These factors may lower your vibrational rate, and that will lessen the productivity of the session.

- It's not unusual to feel tired after a writing session, especially when you are new to the process. This usually lessens the more you write, as you become accustomed to operating in an altered state for longer periods of time.

- If you do not know what to ask, put it in the hands of the Divine and ask for a message. You may have something in particular in mind—Source may have something better.

- Watch for synchronicities and messages that will begin to appear after you start writing. They may appear in music, in a book, a television program, in a movie, or through a casual comment. These are supplemental confirmations of the message you received in your writings.

- Always say thank you!

It is not necessary to master all twelve steps before attempting to do soul writing, but it is worth noting that incorporating each of these practices is helpful in achieving a deeper level of inspired writing. While Cayce no doubt would agree that each step should be heeded, he did not want the writer to forget the most important reason for doing inspirational writing.

The field of activity in which thou art engaged is well. Thy writing and thy meditations are good, if these are kept in that way of putting the stress where the stress is due, giving the credit not to self, not to others, not to the "powers that be" but to Him, who is the Creator, the Maker, remembering, without Him there was not anything made that was made. And He gives it to thee. What will ye do with same (2800-2)?

CHAPTER FIVE

Soul Writing
for Past-Life Exploration

Past-life research, exploration, and education has been a passion of mine for years. Even when I knew relatively little about it, on a subliminal level I readily accepted the premise that my current life was merely the continuation of a long list of previous lifetimes.

Although I considered myself a devout Roman Catholic and attended parochial school for twelve years, I nonetheless always had a problem with the idea that we only had one life, and if we didn't follow the rules, we would be doomed to eternal damnation. I could not reconcile the idea of a loving and just God with hell and brimstone preaching, so I readily questioned the logic of this dogma. The priests and nuns at St. Barbara High School were not amused. One nun labeled me an atheist. One priest said I was looking for an emotional religion, and religion, he said, was intellectual. I could find all the answers I needed if I would just read the recommended texts. I never had a detention throughout my school years until my senior year in high school when I posed these questions with fervor. It was then that every time I raised my hand, I was never called upon, but silently handed a detention slip. I learned to stop asking questions aloud, but that did not deter me from continuing to post the questions on my mind's bulletin board in the hope they'd be read by some passing angel.

During my teens, I began reading books by Ruth Montgomery and Jess Stearn, and it was then that I started reading about Edgar Cayce. The first book I read on reincarnation was *The Search for Bridey Murphy,* by Morey Bernstein, which originally was published in 1956. The book mesmerized me, as did the philosophy of reincarnation. Finally, everything made sense in the context of a just God and a harmonious Universe, where every deed—good, bad, and indifferent—was recorded and dealt with on a karmic scale. Karma made much more sense to me than sin. Living by the law of Karma, if I accidentally ate meat on Friday and then had the misfortune of being hit by a bus, I would not be condemned to the fiery pits of hell for all eternity. Actually, looking at the bigger picture, eating meat on Friday was immaterial as far as my soul's growth was concerned. Did God really care if I ate a hamburger on Friday?

I suspect each one of us has that one book that is the key to unlocking the door that connects us to the All That Is. *Bridey Murphy* did that for me. After that, I developed an insatiable appetite for metaphysical studies. My parents were oblivious to my new interest, and had they known, I doubt they would have objected in the least. They didn't think things like that were important. As long as I was within sight and did not get into trouble, they left me alone to pursue my interests.

Once in a while, however, my father would say something exceedingly profound—something you would not expect from a truck driver whose daily route took him into the roughest neighborhoods in Chicago. I always thought of my father as a lost soul—an artist with enormous talent who was wasting away in a job that paid well but drained his spirit. I remember when he was in one of his rare philosophical moods, he quoted Napoleon Hill: "What the mind of man can conceive and believe, it can achieve." It was an odd thing for a worn-out trucker to say to his teenage daughter, but it made a lasting impression on me. I remember applying that to reincarnation and asked him if he believed in past lives. He was noncommittal but did not rule it out.

While I was a casual student of reincarnation, I did not pursue it with passion until 1987 when I got my first confirmation of an eighteenth-century past life in Virginia. Like most novice seekers of esoteric truths, I turned to others for answers. Being a member of the A.R.E. Heartland Region core team at that time enabled me to meet some of the leading professionals in the field of past-life research. All were interested in my story and made suggestions on how to get to the core issues of that life, but no one gave me the tools I needed to find the answers I so desperately wanted.

Then by chance, in an effort to get help with something totally unrelated—my commercial writing—I ordered a writer's subconscious programming tape from Dick Sutphen called "Start Writing Now." I had not worked with a hypnosis tape before, so I wasn't sure what I was getting into, but the idea of writing in an altered state intrigued me. It never occurred to me that I would use it for past-life exploration.

As I listened to the tape, Sutphen suggested creating a mental movie in which I perceived myself already writing, to create a vivid fantasy in which I was successfully expressing myself in words. He suggested the movie was real and asked me to play the role, play the part, and experience every detail in my mind. If I did this, he said, my desires would be communicated to my subconscious mind, which would assist me by generating circumstances to create my programmed reality.

Mental movie? Play the role? The floodgates opened. When he said to begin the visualization now, my mental movie began:

It was evening. I saw a woman who looked a bit like me when I was much younger, but the dimness of the room prevented me from observing her closely enough to determine her identity. From what I could see, she appeared to be around twenty years of age; she had long, straight, black hair that cascaded down her back. She timidly stood at the top of the stairs, dressed in a loose-fitting, long, white cotton shift with a white, lace-trimmed nightcap on her head. With only a candle to illuminate her way, she cautiously began to descend, looking to see if anyone was awake. I sensed that she did not want anyone to discover her roaming the house at such a late hour.

When she reached the bottom of the stairs, she lit another candle on a nearby desk. She pulled out the chair, slowly seated herself, took out a journal that was tucked in the folds of her skirt, and reached for a quill pen. The moment she began to write, the pen that I had poised over my own journal began to move. Excerpts from that notation follow:

This summer was especially beautiful. The flowers in the garden were resplendent in their color and fragrance. I so enjoyed walking among them. It kept the memory of him ever near to me. I could feel his presence. I could hear his voice. Such a comfort in these difficult times of separation. I know in my heart he is mine. He has always

 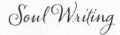

known in his that I am his. There is no denying it to each other. But there is always that pain . . . I am alone in the garden just as I am alone in this life. A prisoner of my emotions . . . Would that times be different. But I must face life as it is given to me now. How fortunate I am to be a part of his life. What circumstances lend us to be together in this tragic yet wondrous relationship? I walk alone yet he is near. And I know I am so much a part of him as he is me. Silent lovers in this sea of secrecy. Drowning in the silence. Unable to laugh. Unable to cry. Caught in the everlasting emotional tide that comes in and engulfs me. . . .

This went on for another four pages until the writing stopped, then a hesitation, and then a date was written: *September 7, 1793.*

Huh? 1793? I was jolted awake, as if startled by the thud of a large book falling to the floor. *What in the world is this?* I asked myself in a very judgmental tone. It read like a page in an embarrassingly sophomoric historical romance novel. I knew I didn't write like that. I had *never* written like that. I wanted to be inspired to write better press releases and brochures, not this trite stuff about flowers in a garden. *Who in the world is doing this writing? It certainly isn't me.* Yet what was it that Dick Sutphen said at the end of the visualization exercise? "You have just seen your reality." My reality—or someone else's?

Thinking it a fluke, I decided to try again the following night. I played the tape and once again during the visualization exercise, there was that same young woman at the top of the stairs, wearing the same clothes, carrying the candle as she gingerly walked down the stairs, seating herself at the same desk, reaching for the same quill pen, and once again commencing the writing. And as before, as she wrote, so did I.

Breakfast was quiet. Some disturbing news arrived last night . . .
I did not hear it all as I was busy with our son, but I knew it was
a serious discussion as my beloved was pacing the floor most of the
night. Even I was unable to console him. . . .

Again, four pages describing in great detail an event in the life of this mysterious woman. This time the diary entry—for lack of a better term—was dated April 30, 1794. I again awoke from my reverie, not so much because of being surprised by the date, but because I knew the session was over.

The following night, the same thing happened. The journal entry was dated May 8, 1795. And on it went. I received several more journal entries over the course of the next few days. The final one was dated June 1, 1798. It had a happier tone to it as "she" described the events of the day, but a sense of sadness still enveloped the entry as she expressed her love for a man apparently who could never acknowledge her.

What had I stumbled onto? The writer's subconscious programming tape was not developed as a past-life tool, but after these journal entries, I could not help but wonder if in fact I was that woman on the staircase who did her clandestine journal writing in the middle of the night. I did not have to wait long for an answer. I received that confirmation the next day, when the journal entry I received was directed at me and was dated that very night: December 16, 1990. I soon realized that my past-life personality was attempting to communicate with my present-life personality.

The entry was written both in first and second person, so it was confusing to follow. "She" referred to me by name, saying she incarnated as the present entity, Joanne. Then she wrote:

She is so like me, yet she disbelieves. I would not believe so easily.
We are one. She feels my passion. I share that with her in dreams, in

 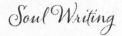

songs, in moving pictures. She remembers. No more passion in this lifetime, sweet Joanne. Just all these confusing memories for you to sort through. We would not have planned this now if we did not think you could handle it. If we did not think you were ready. You remember me but you are much more than the number of years I walked the face of the Earth. We are here in assistance to help you to remember it all—all of the evolutionary lives you've lived—to prepare you for the great work that is ahead. Now we must get beyond this—beyond this incessant disbelief of yours. I know you are saddened by what you perceive you are missing in life. I share in that sadness but I also rejoice because so much more lies ahead of you. It won't be easy but the world is finally ready to hear the message. It has taken all these centuries to reach this point. Remember your purpose. Go beyond your life as me. Go beyond them all. Gather them together like fragile flowers in your basket. Breathe deep the splendid hues and remember. Remember it all—you have the ability. Go beyond the doubt. We are with you always. I, as a part of your higher self, for that is where I now reside to give you comfort and courage and encouragement. Tap into those memories as only you can. No one else can do it for you. So many will be healed by your words and we—all of us who are you—will rest at evening's call knowing it is done. Knowing all is as it should be. You write about no limits to what can be done if you believe in yourself. Believe, Joanne, dear child believe, for within you lies the key that will unlock the final door of your servitude and free all of us to soar in the Universe, touching the earth with an iridescent light unseen before. For one soul freed brings freedom to all others. One soul freed brings freedom to all. Free us, Joanne. And you.

I was stunned. This entry turned the tables on me as the writer. Instead of me initiating contact with my soul, this time my soul was writing to me. Some part of my past was resurfacing and using the written word to paint a picture of a life that existed some two hundred years earlier. Now I understood that I could go into an altered state of consciousness and use this form of writing to access past-life information—information that came from my soul, not information spoon fed to me by individuals who thought they knew more about my past life than I did.

I knew that memories of previous lives are buried deep within one's soul. I also knew enough about past-life work to know that unexplained thoughts, feelings, and fears could be explained by accessing a past-life memory and understanding its karmic implications. By using soul writing, that information was readily accessible.

Knowing I am the sum of all my previous incarnations, I concluded that all of the information about who I was, what issues I faced, lessons I learned, unfinished business, etc., was contained within my soul's memory. I reasoned that by getting in touch with that aspect of me through soul writing, I could tap into that storehouse of past-life memories. Using the writer's programming tape, I had stumbled on a way to submerge my current personality (conscious self) and invite my past personality (subconscious self) to emerge and, through writing, record events from "her" lifetime in "her" own words.

With that as my intent, I began a nightly ritual of meditation, visualization, and prayer. Since I knew I was dealing with an eighteenth-century lifetime, I created an environment as conducive to that time period as possible. I worked by candlelight, played classical music in the background, and wrote with a fountain pen. To my astonishment, it worked. At first I received information in diary format, but the dates skipped around in no particular order from 1792 to 1807. Each entry contained a fascinating peek at my prior lifetime, but provided no cohesive storyline for me to follow.

At some point, the dizzying time hopping stopped, and

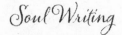

the writing became very focused with a day-by-day accounting of what happened in that life from July 1802 to January 1803. The process took years, and I ultimately ended up with a six hundred–page manuscript. I made a halfhearted attempt to get it published, pawning it off as historical fiction, but to no avail. It remains unpublished to this day, and that is all right with me, for I look upon it as my greatest soul writing accomplishment. Who knows? Someday it may find its way to a bookstore near you!

In the meantime, I have found that using soul writing to explore past lives is a tool that can help answer questions on myriad subjects. In the fall of 2010, I developed a workshop called "Finding Your Soul's Purpose Using Meditation, Past-Life Regression, and Soul Writing." In it, I conduct a past-life regression to assist participants to find the lifetime in which they could acquire positive resources that they could apply to their lives today, as well as discover the negative imprints that were keeping them from doing their soul's work.

As a follow-up to those exercises, I include a soul writing session in which I ask the question: "What is your soul's purpose?" Participants found that the writing session expanded on the regression, clarifying the source of the positive resources and negative imprints from previous lifetimes. By exploring those past lives through soul writing, they were able to go back and review the circumstances that initiated those positive and negative imprints, considering their implications in their lives today, and make whatever changes were needed to cash in on the resources and reprogram the negative imprint for a more positive outcome.

All information about past lives is stored in the Akashic Records. Therefore, when you enter a state of transcendental meditation, you can enter the Hall of Records and read the sojourn of your soul. This is not something reserved for a gifted few. You can go to that library, pull down your book, and read in vivid detail the account of any lifetime you had, and then record what you learned through soul writing.

You can also do as I did and submerge your present personality's consciousness, and for that writing session allow your past-life personality's consciousness to share its autobiography. Because we are the sum of all we were before, it stands to reason that somewhere within our souls is a record of each of our past lives. Therefore, if those memories remain within the soul, they can be recalled and provide you with memories of a life lived long ago.

You may be thinking—isn't this courting possession? No. Tapping into your previous lifetime's memories does not mean you are contacting attached entities. The energies that express themselves through writing are not struggling to take over your life so that they can live again. What you are tapping into are memories—as real as those of your current life's childhood or teen years or of someone dear to you that you knew years ago. The soul's memory is eternal, and it transcends the experiences you have lived through in your current body. The memory remains intact within the soul, willing to remain silent unless needed.

For someone like me, for whom the veil was lifted long ago, I sense no passage of time from one lifetime to the other. As far as I am concerned, they are all one. I do not see life—or eternity—as compartmentalized into the past, present, and future, so I am not one who embraces the "live in the present moment" philosophy. That would require seeing the journey of the soul in a linear fashion, separated into moments that occurred, are occurring, or will occur. For me, it is simply a continuum. It has no beginning, no middle, and no end.

This is an area of past-life work that I find fascinating—to find a way to enable people to awaken their soul's memories

and recall previous lifetimes so that they can see for themselves that the soul does not die, that there is a natural flow from one life to the next. Imagine a world in which people did this. How different would our civilization be if people understood themselves better by seeing the road that led them to the here and now; a road on which they were every race, gender, religion, and nationality. There would be no sense of separation, for we would see that we are all linked, one to the other.

A soul's existence does not start and stop in each lifetime. When you are born, you do not come into this world empty handed. You come in with tools, with talents, skills, attitudes, issues, etc., that you earned in previous lifetimes. Those abilities are stored in your soul's bank account, to be withdrawn whenever needed.

Is it so strange, then, to know that by entering a state of meditation, connecting to the All That Is, you could ask a question about something in your life that makes no sense to you now, but when explained in the context of a previous life makes all the sense in the world? That is the benefit of soul writing.

Ask a question about any aspect of your being. Why do you struggle with friendships? Why don't you feel love when it is given to you? Why are you inclined to attract abusive people? Why does music come so naturally to you? Why do you have such a deep affection for your grandmother? Why do you feel you are unwanted? Why do people naturally gravitate to you?

The answers may be in another lifetime—a lifetime in which you were neglectful of your friends. You rejected love. You were abusive. You were a great singer or composer. You saved your grandmother's life. You pushed people away. You helped others.

Ask your soul why—and wait for the answer. It will come and in so doing answer many of those questions that have been gnawing away at you for years. What a gift that is for any soul willing to connect to Spirit; ask the question and then allow the answer to come forth through your own hand.

CHAPTER SIX

Soul Writing to Enhance Psychic Abilities

Individuals seek psychics for answers to questions concerning their mission in life, their relationship to others, what is in store for them in the future, and who they were in a past life. They ask about their finances, their career, their deceased loved ones, the meaning of their dreams, and their latest ailments. They go to channelers, healers, and readers because they believe that only these people possess the God-given talent to provide those answers. The same could be said for soul writing. But what these seekers forget is that, as Cayce says, "all answers lie within." That is why learning how to do soul writing and applying it to one's life can open doors to finding those much-sought-after answers on one's own. Best of all, there's no middleman, and it doesn't cost anything but an investment of your time.

Cayce said we are all born with psychic abilities to a certain degree. "EVERY entity has clairvoyant, mystic, psychic powers . . . The intuitional, which is both clairvoyant and psychic, is the higher development . . ." (1500-4).

Unfortunately, as children we were not encouraged to develop these abilities, so they remained dormant. Soul writing—like other psychic abilities, talents, and artistic skills—is a part of us waiting to be developed.

Meditation, relaxation, and creative visualization are essential elements in the process of soul writing. Any one of these, used alone or in consort with one another, enables one to achieve a higher level of mind and tap into one's inherent psychic abilities.

To connect to the All That Is creates a thread between soul and Spirit—a silver thread that is a direct link to all the wisdom of the Universe. Therefore, when you enter that place of inner tranquility and peacefulness, you can access the ability to see, to hear, to feel, and to perceive all levels of knowing. Senses are heightened in this state, and a counsel of wise and loving energies are available to provide answers in whatever format works best for you at that moment in time.

Can you recall a time when you were in a self-imposed reverie when something of a psychic nature manifested? Once I was sitting alone on my family room floor with my eyes closed, listening to soothing music through headphones so as not to disturb my sleeping children. After some time, I involuntarily took in a deep breath, and suddenly the scent of my late grandmother's perfume filled my nostrils. It took me by surprise; I opened my eyes, half-expecting to see her in the room. Despite her physical absence, I could feel her presence. My grandmother and I shared a close and loving bond, and the moment I smelled that perfume, I was overcome with emotion, remembering how much I missed her. At the same time, I was strangely comforted by her mystical presence in the room. I am sure that had anyone walked into the room at that moment, they would not have sensed any of what I was experiencing. It was a psychic gift meant only for me.

Music is my connection to Spirit, and I have used it often in my reveries to reach a higher state of mind. When I had my past life center—PLEXUS—I rented it to other like-minded souls, including a Course in Miracles group that met there weekly. Prior to their arrival one night, I came in early to set up the room. When I finished, I dimmed the lights, turned on meditative music, and sat on the floor with my back against the wall. I closed my eyes and allowed the quietness of Spirit to permeate the room. I don't remember how much time passed, but when I opened my eyes, the instructor for the course was standing before me with a gentle smile on his face. He said he was reveling in the energy of the room. Having experienced the room many times before, he attributed the change in the energy to whatever I was doing and asked how I did it. I smiled and replied that I really did not know *how* I did it. I just knew that at this moment in time, this was where I wanted to be, and I felt in perfect harmony and alignment with every other soul.

Have you ever visualized yourself in a specific career or relationship? Have you seen yourself in a different home, perhaps in another state or even another country? Have you seen family members surrounding you who did not look familiar but you sensed were yours? Have you pictured yourself doing a specific activity that you don't do now, such as hiking or playing the piano or teaching?

The process that brings forward these images is the same energy that you put forth when you prepare to work with deep soul writing. If I'd had paper and pen with me when my grandmother's spirit entered the room, or when the energy at PLEXUS shifted during my meditation, I am certain I would have received an extraordinary written message.

It is this preparation—this tuning in—that opens the door to achieving profound levels of psychic ability. For some it means awakening clairaudience abilities; that is, actually hearing messages from your higher self. After all, the same Source that writes, also talks. Once I learned to meditate and surrender myself to the flow of information coming to me through writing, I began hearing the messages in my mind, especially during long walks. These solitary strolls became a moving meditation in which ideas formulated that I had not considered in a conscious state. At first I thought this was just the normal function of the brain, generating thoughts and ideas, but then I realized that much of what I was "hearing" was in the form of divine guidance. It wasn't just a brazen— *why not do this*—kind of information. It was more a gentle nudging to do something I was resisting but which ultimately would lead to a leap in my soul's growth.

A good example of how this process works happened to me a few years ago. During my daily walks, I began to get messages about reconnecting with a once-dear friend whom I had not spoken to in years. We had been close for fourteen years, but then we each entered difficult phases in our lives during which changes began happening at a rapid rate. Because these shifts in our consciousness were so radical, it shook the foundation of our friendship. We tried to be supportive of each other, but soon it became obvious that we had opposing opinions of what was best for each other. After a while, our friendship ended, each feeling the other was responsible for its demise.

For the longest time, I mourned her absence in my life, and I tried repeatedly to understand what had gone wrong. What was my part in it? What lesson was being presented? Was there any chance we could ever be friends again?

I used soul writing as a prayer to help me come to terms with the loss of this friendship and to find those answers I so desperately sought. The responses I received assured me that all was not lost and that we would be friends again, but I had a difficult time believing this. Rather than follow the advice that my higher self was giving me through my soul writing sessions—to be patient and not give up on her—I went on with life thinking that it was futile to continue thinking about the "what ifs" of that relationship.

Although the written messages persisted in trying to shift my consciousness, I chose to ignore them. That's when Spirit decided to try another course of action. Nearly every day on my walks, my old friend would pop into my mind. I would see her clearly and, in the silence of those walks, would converse with her, sharing with her all the love and affection I still had in my heart for her. Over and over I would hear that conversation during those walks, guided by words I was sure were coming from my higher self because they were gentle, kind, and loving as opposed to accusatory or blaming. They were simply—I love you, I miss you, I would welcome another chance.

Eventually I grew tired of the same conversation, and I knew I had to do something about it. It was obvious I would get no peace until I followed my inner guidance to try to reconnect with her.

With that in mind, I entered my reverie and wrote a letter to her. In it I shared that for over a year during my walks, I had been encouraged by Spirit to contact her. I also admitted that I had hesitated in doing so for fear of how she would react. I told her that despite the time that had passed, I hoped we now were both in a place where we could think of the past with love rather than regret. I told her of the changes in my life and of the soulful journey I had been on since our friendship ended.

I understood that only a soul who truly loved me would have agreed to come into my life to help me resolve karmic issues and to grow in love and forgiveness, and that rather than being embittered or resentful, I felt nothing but gratitude to her as she had come into my life in loving service. I thanked her and told her how much she had meant to me, and that now when I thought of her, I felt great comfort, remembering what a good friend she had been. I hoped she thought the same of me. Apparently she did, because she responded, and we were able to resume our friendship once more as if it had never ended. I thank Spirit for that, because without the words I received through soul writing and the messages I heard during my walks, I never would have taken the step to repair the wounds from that relationship.

Soul writing opens psychic doors in ways we cannot imagine. For those who learn to make the connection with Spirit through the written word, clairvoyant (seeing) abilities increase. You can visualize people, places, and things that aren't in your physical space at that moment in time. In doing so, you can fast forward and see what lies ahead, as I did on my walks when I saw my estranged friend with me once more.

This ability cannot be underestimated when it comes to creating transformational shifts in your thinking. Once when I was in a very dark place, I was lying in bed thinking that I would be better off not being in the world any longer. While I never seriously considered suicide, I was experiencing that dark night of the soul, and I admit to entertaining many bleak "what if" thoughts.

That particular night, I felt alone and alienated from everyone. I was also feeling very sorry for myself, wondering why I was constantly struggling with issues of acceptance and approval. It seemed that no matter what I did, these issues

continued to plague me, and the consequences were painful and seemingly never ending.

After a while, I began to drift off, and just as I reached that twilight state between sleep and wakefulness, I opened my eyes slightly and saw nine beings shimmering in an almost blinding white light. They surrounded my bed: four to my left; four to my right; and one standing at the foot of the bed. The one at the foot was very handsome—appearing to be in his early twenties, with blond hair, piercing blue eyes, and radiating a light greater than the others. They did not say a word, and I did not try to communicate with them, but something astounding happened in that silence as I gazed upon them. I no longer felt alone. The despair I had been feeling left, and I was suddenly filled with a sense of purpose and determination. I fell asleep and awoke with a new attitude that propelled me forward. It is these same nine energies that write with me today.

Besides clairaudience and clairvoyance, for those who work with soul writing, there is a marked increase in clairsentience (intuition) as well. Your senses are heightened, and you begin to feel things internally. You are more keenly aware of your gut feelings about someone or something. My inspired writings often talk of some hidden aspect of a relationship, offering insights that I could not comprehend in a conscious state. Sometimes it is a red flag, advising me not to become involved with someone or some cause. Other times that same intuitive sense provides a calming reassurance about a fledgling relationship, giving me the green light to move forward.

Dream interpretation is another area where soul writing can expand your psychic senses to find answers. Dreams are filled with symbols and seemingly disjointed images. There are so many confusing messages that it is easy to misinterpret the dream's true meaning. By entering an altered state and asking one's higher self for clarification of a dream's message, detailed explanations of symbols, individuals, relationships, locales, and experiences will be forthcoming. This enables the dreamer to understand and integrate the message.

In January 2011, I had a dream about being in a small, octagonal shed that had no furniture in it whatsoever—it was just an empty space. A large body of water surrounded the shed. When I opened the door, I could see that the water was rising and the waves were moving rapidly in one direction. The shed did not move against the onslaught of the waves. It was as if I were standing on a rock in the middle of the Colorado River rapids. Everything was moving at great speeds around me, but as long as I remained inside the shed, I felt no movement whatsoever.

I decided to ask my higher self to interpret the dream, even though its symbolism was fairly elementary, and I could have figured it out for myself. Still, I don't believe I would have written the explanation in quite this manner, nor would it have had as great an impact on me had I written it knowing that I was not connected to Spirit.

My dear child, we are with you in love and in light. Within that building you may have felt safe, but you were nonetheless trapped, a prisoner behind its walls while outside the world was rapidly passing you by. You remained stationery, not able to move while you looked out at the rushing water. You could not see a beginning or an end to the waters—as if the shed itself was an island. While you were not fearful, a part of you longed to jump into the water to see where it would take you, for the water represented power, adventure, moving on to an unknown destination, which you found exciting. You would have to jump into the water alone, for there was no boat or others around to assist. While the waters appeared threatening and capable of drowning you instantly, the thought of death never crossed your mind. You did not want to stay on your island. You wanted to leave—yet in this dream you stayed in the safe little shed, preferring to wait it out until such time as the water abated. Two aspects of yourself were at odds—that part of you that is fearful of branching out on your own, leaving the safety and security of the life you now have in favor of one with limitless possibilities, but definite uncertainties and the possibility of being overcome by the high waves or drowning in the churning depths of the growing rapids. Yet it was the latter that excited you and sparked your interest. You were so sure everything would be all right if you stepped out the door, yet you remained inside. So is the choice in your life now. Stay in the relative safety and security of your life—empty as the shed itself—or take the leap into the rapids that will take you to your next destination. This is the meaning of the dream and the issue your subconscious wrestles with at this moment in your evolution.

I knew instantly that the reference was to a previous lifetime and to a particular person in my life at that time. It was symbolically linking the two, showing that I am facing many of the same issues as before—to stay with someone in a place where I felt cared for but empty inside, or to take a leap of faith into uncharted territory to change my lot in life. As my writing session so eloquently put it, it is indeed an issue my subconscious wrestles with at this moment in time.

Bobbie Ann Pimm is the author of *Notes from a Dreamer . . . on Dreaming: A Personal Journey in Dream Interpretation* and a member of the Atlantic University faculty. Bobbie is also the "Bobbie" who is one of the eight participants I refer to in my inspirational writing research project (see chapter 12).

"It seems that I have been using 'soul writing' for many years before you introduced the term to me, in recalling and understanding dreams," she told me. "In the morning when

I first awake, I lay still for several minutes, recapturing the imagery of my dreams. At times there's only a snippet or two, and yet when I pick up my pen and start writing, I find words and recall images that initially were not there. I stop several minutes later and am amazed at how much I've written. If I then stay in that moment and read over what I've written, I continue to use inspired writing to seek deeper connections and an understanding of the dream."

With dreams, as with other tools for growth, the extraordinary power of soul writing is its ability to expand our psychic abilities and enable us to tap into our sixth sense. You don't have to be tested to determine whether you are psychic or not. Each of us has the ability and can use clairvoyance, clairaudience, or clairsentience as one of many avenues to find answers to life's questions. It can be done by simply entering a peaceful place, asking the question, and then listening to that still, small voice within for the answer. It's very much like typing in a question on a search engine. Millions of other people may be doing the exact same thing at the exact same time, but somehow, someway, we get a direct line to the Universe's Help Desk where answers are there for the asking.

Now, this isn't to say that if you are not cautious, or if you don't take this seriously, you may find a mischievous spirit on the other end of the line. Case in point: I received a psychic message to look for a particular book at the Theosophical Society's Quest Bookstore in Wheaton, Illinois. I was given the title and told this book held answers to a few of my long-standing questions. I was told I would be guided to the book once I got to the store.

Excited at this prospect, I asked a friend to tag along so I could prove to her how guided writing could be used to expand my psychic abilities. When we got to the bookstore, I felt no need to say my usual prayer of protection as I took out my notebook. I suppose I thought I had carte blanche from previous sessions. In any event, I stood in the middle of the store, pen poised on my notebook, awaiting instructions. They came almost immediately, telling me to go to a specific aisle. I did so and then poised the pen again over the notebook. Once more the writing told me to go to yet another aisle, and I did, awaiting the next instruction. I was told to move to the left of that aisle, which I did. I was then instructed to scan the second shelf from the top where I would find this book. Of course, the book was not there, and when I approached a member of the staff to ask if the title had been backordered, she said there was no such title in their catalog. I felt foolish, but I did learn my lesson. When it came to extolling my psychic abilities, that was the last time I attempted any kind of dog-and-pony show using guided writing.

CHAPTER SEVEN

Soul Writing in Other Art Forms

The process—a ritual-like sequence of steps—for doing soul writing contains many of the same elements used in other artistic forms. The creative process as a whole follows a familiar pattern. Artists using this process may meditate prior to beginning their work. They may follow a ritual of lighting candles, playing relaxing music, doing deep breathing exercises, and saying a prayer that their hand be guided by divine inspiration.

Thus they start the process of "inspirational painting" or "inspirational composing" in much the same way that a writer begins to put sentences together. This process enables them to find a starting point, or it may help them to visualize the finished piece through "inspirational visioning." It also can be used to get unstuck should they feel blocked when their creative energy no longer flows.

As a stream-of-consciousness technique, the process used in soul writing frees the imagination and gently nudges the writer in a direction that he may not have otherwise considered. Because it is an intuitive process, the same methods used in soul writing can be transferred to the visual arts and serve as the foundation for a much greater, more refined piece of art.

Regardless of the artistic genre, the source of inspiration for writers is the same as it is for other artists. Ideas come while walking in nature, in the shower, or lying in bed staring at the ceiling. Tapping into a universal consciousness, artists experience free-flowing ideas that resonate with their own. If—as I believe it does—all inspiration comes from Spirit, then accessing that higher vibration kick starts ideas that translate into creative expression no matter what the genre.

For writers who wish to use soul writing to express themselves in forms of writing other than prose, the method is the same. On rare occasions when I have entered a meditative state with the intention of obtaining guidance on a particular topic, the response has come in the form of a poem. I do not write poems, nor do I especially enjoy that medium; therefore, when I meditate only to find myself writing a free-flowing poem, I tend to sit up and take notice. This definitely is not coming from my conscious self. The energy feels different from when I receive guidance in the form of prose.

I began producing inspirational poetry in 1989. Once again, the ability manifested when I least expected it. One evening I found myself paging through my favorite book of quotations. I decided to write the ones I liked best in a journal. As I did, I got a strong urge to meditate on the meaning of a quotation and allow a supplemental verse to come through using inspirational writing.

One of the first quotes I read was: "What is human is immortal." I took several deep breaths, said a prayer of protection, and meditated on those five words. A short time later, the following response came through:

> *Death is but a temporary transition*
> *from this world to the next.*
> *Know in your heart that*
> *you will be together again . . .*
> *To laugh . . .*
> *To cry . . .*
> *To love.*
> *As you have before,*
> *so you will again.*

The thought came to me that this would be a comforting sympathy card, but I quickly dismissed it and went on to meditate on the next quote: "If a man is worth knowing at all, he is worth knowing well."

Again I went through the same meditative process, and again words formed in response to the quote:

> *And you, my friend, I have known before.*
> *In countless ages past.*
> *In the great light of God.*
> *Through adversity and sublime*
> *I have known you*
> *as I know you now.*
> *I am with you always*
> *in love*
> *and in Light.*

The thought "birthday card" came into my mind, but again I dismissed it as being silly, as I still could not grasp that I was writing this way. Out of curiosity, however, I went on to the next quote: "'Tis always morning somewhere in the world."

To which the reply was:

> *A bright warm sky*
> *is burning in your heart.*
> *No need to search outward.*
> *No need to look out.*
> *Be as one with sky and wind,*
> *but know all answers*
> *lie within.*

"That's interesting," I told myself, wondering how long I could keep this up. Rudyard Kipling provided the next quote: "Yours is the Earth and everything that's in it."

The response:

> *Are we not all one*
> *part of a greater force*
> *from which stems all creation?*
> *Share in that which is your birthright.*
> *Rejoice in the magnificence of the dawn.*
> *And know you are of it all.*

These were basic metaphysical concepts—the idea that all answers lie within and that humanity is connected to a greater whole. Growing weary, I decided for my last attempt I would turn to the Bible for inspiration and chose a quotation from Ecclesiastes 9:10: "Whatsoever thy hand findeth to do, do it with thy might."

To which the response was:

You have it within you
to achieve a greatness
limited only by the
boundaries of your
belief in yourself.
I believe in you.

This would make a wonderful graduation card, I thought—the idea finally sinking in that Spirit was providing me with a whole new genre to get my writing out to the public and, in doing so, offer inspirational messages of hope and transformation.

Over the next few days, the process continued until I had twenty-five more quotations and responses. Pursuing the idea that these sentiments would make powerful inspirational greeting cards, I set about to produce the cards. They did not sell as I had hoped. Although financially unsuccessful, they were creatively very successful. I entered "What is human is immortal" in the Third Annual International Greeting Card Association Award Competition—the greeting card industry's equivalent of the Academy Awards. It was selected as one of six in the world as a finalist for that year's LOUIE Awards; chosen for its "creative excellence." Although it did not win first place, it received critical acclaim.

As it turned out, I would not get another poem from Spirit for six years. It was the summer after I moved to Virginia. During my evening meditation, I received this unexpected poem:

My dear child we are with you always in love and in light.
The seeker of Truth comes before you.
Will you recognize his soul?
Will you answer his call?
Be not afraid of what lies ahead
for fear and sorrow are not your stead.
Take heed the warnings of the past
for to find true love that lasts
is but a short distance from your door.
Once found—can you want for more?
Another day, another time is done;
For you, it is the rising of the sun.
Be brave and continue on the path,
for ahead of you will lay the wrath
of one who seeks to block your way.
Best be cautious to rule the day.
Ever so careful must your steps be
for power to be set free.
The gracious one who made your soul
will be with you as all unfolds.
Loving child, be true,
for yet another important clue
is played before you to recall
and once discovered, you will have it all.
Now do not allow our message to wait
for someone else to decipher at the gate.
It is not a game we play dear heart;
It is a rhyme with many parts.

The answer to your question lies
in someone else's eyes.
Be ready and open to accept
the one who will help you to forget.
For all as promised will be real
as soon as you are open and can feel.
The love that has eluded you thus far
will soon arrive not by car
but by plane at the port
where once a ship did sail.
The sea is quiet but for a while
awaiting the vessel that will make you smile.
So do not falter in your resolve
for all problems shall soon be solved.
Rest now in quiet thought
and be at peace, for all is naught
as you would believe it to be.
A new development you shall soon see
and in the end, a great joy.
For coming to you is a very special boy
who was so young when last your way
but now is a man as you see him today.
Our promise to you shall be kept
to soothe all the times you wept.
Prepare you now with rest and sleep
for tomorrow comes quickly and this
one you will want to keep.

Friends who read this poem were astounded at the specificity of the message. Who was this strange man who was coming by plane? Someone who would initiate a transformation in my life?

Part of the poem is true. In the coming years I did encounter "the wrath of one who seeks to block your way." As for the man on the plane, if I did meet this person, it left no lasting memory. Then again, in the spirit world there is no time, and it could be that this person is yet to reveal himself. The cryptic nature of the message was intriguing, but I made no serious effort to decipher its meaning.

A week later, I received a combination poetry/prose message. Its intent was to provide answers to the ongoing question I raised about the source of the guidance that came through my soul writing. The writing continued to yield veiled messages.

My dear child we are with you always in love and light. As it is answers you seek so boldly, we are ready with replies. The energies working through you are ascended masters. Spirit names will be revealed to you, as each share a message at a later time, for a signature will be placed at the end of each message so you will know with whom you are communicating. Messages such as the one you are receiving now are a joint communiqué and as such reflect the combined consciousness of all who seek to guide your way.

You say you are ready and well you are.
To see and hear one cannot ask
for the secret to the knowledge lies in the past.
A crimson color did you wear
with golden ribbon in your hair
in a time where ancient gods did rise

and plant their wisdom in your eyes.
So now you wonder what is the task
that brings you here at last?
Why wonder what is so real?
Why ask that it be revealed
when in your heart you already know
the whys, wherefores, whens, and woes?
You have always known it's true
why you are here and what you are to do.
So as it unfolds before your eyes
do not sit back and act surprised,
but seize the day and all it gives.
For to do so, one will truly live
in the shining love of Master Mind
who has made you of His kind.
Go forth, dear heart, make haste,
for you are now well past the starting gate.
To thine own self be true
and we will see what we can do
to hurry along the pre-ordained plan
so you can be on with teaching fellow man
the wisdom of the ancient ones.
For it has now just begun
to unfold for thee
and your new family.

This writing session offered hints of what appears to be an ancient past life. It also implied that the work I was to do in this lifetime was connected to the work I did in one or more past lives, but that is a common theme in past-life recall. I already had a sense of what I was here to do in this life—as they stated—but I had not clearly defined how that work would unfold.

Occasionally poetry would take on a specific form with repetitious first lines and measured stanzas, such as this one I received in July 1997:

> *Be not fearful as you venture on*
> *to find the place you are to settle upon.*
> *For in the choosing comes the flight*
> *to a place where you will embrace the night.*
>
> *Be not fearful as you venture on*
> *to find the answers you believe are gone.*
> *For in the search there is a light*
> *that shines upon you in the endless fight.*
>
> *Be not fearful as you venture on*
> *and make thy home aside the pond.*
> *For in the shadows lurks the key*
> *that opens the door to your eternity.*
>
> *Be not fearful as you venture on*
> *leaving behind that which served you well.*
> *For having the courage to go on*
> *will give you endless rewards you deserve so well.*
>
> *Now rest and do what is right*
> *For our love is with you now and through this night.*

Although I received this message many years ago, it continues to give me hope, as it alludes to two life desires that I have not yet achieved—"thy home aside the pond" and "leaving behind that which served you so well" . . . to reap those . . . "endless rewards you deserve so well." I continue toward that goal.

As stated earlier, in reading the volumes of messages I received through guided writing, the main difference between those that manifest as poems versus prose is that the poems are always cryptic in nature, whereas the essays are clearer. Soul writing is usually fairly straightforward. After all, what good is guidance if you can't understand it? While it is true that some prose can be as baffling as the most cryptic of poems, essays generally express their intent in a precise manner and read more like a loving letter from a dear friend than from an unseen mystical prophet.

Every artist seeks his or her Muse because they believe that inspiration that comes from a Higher Source will lift them beyond human limitations and enable them to create something greater than what they could achieve on their own. And that is quite liberating.

As in writing or any other form of guided art, the artist learns to trust the process and get out of the way, allowing whatever comes to mind to materialize on the page or the canvas. Soul writing can blossom into a prize-winning novel or poem; inspirational drawing can become an exceptional piece of art; the inspired playing of an instrument can be the first notes of a moving musical composition. When you begin the process with no preconceived notion of the final outcome and you trust that inspiration will come, you open the door to achieving creativity at its highest level.

CHAPTER EIGHT

Soul Writing to Explore Religious Philosophies

In the summer of 2000, I was thinking about Universal Laws and how they related to the Ten Commandments. I attempted to do research on my own, but was unable to find answers that satisfied my endless list of questions.

It occurred to me that the greatest source for getting answers to spiritual questions is Spirit itself, and the way that I connected to Spirit was through soul writing. I had never used inspirational writing to engage in a philosophical discussion of a specific topic and consequently was not sure what would transpire.

My intent was to focus my writing sessions on Universal Laws, but knowing my interest really centered on how they related to the Ten Commandments, the writings went in that direction. To my astonishment, much of the information I received was something I had never consciously thought about, opening me to a different perspective. It was then that I realized that my thinking was rigid and narrow and that I had much to learn.

Over the years, I had heard that there were anywhere from twenty to fifty Universal Laws, so my first question was straightforward. *How many Universal Laws are there?* The following is what I received in that opening writing session.

The question of how many Universal Laws there are is an interesting one from our perspective because we are not limited by the finite dimensions of time, space, or linear movement. Are there twenty laws or two hundred? You have heard varying numbers. The Creator gave Moses Ten Commandments, yet within these ten, how many laws now appear in your civics books? How many vast interpretations are there—so many and so complex that they end up before that which you call a Supreme Court. Supreme indeed. There is no such thing as Supreme in the eyes of the Creator. You make everything exceedingly complicated when the intent was always simplistic, harmonious Truth.

We would say it is a simple matter to trace each of the thousands of laws you have on the books back to the ten Moses was given. This goes back to what we were saying yesterday regarding taking a Universal Law and reworking it so that it becomes convoluted and in turn becomes a whole new law or a whole new truth. How many varying degrees have you created for "Thou Shalt Not Lie?" We are not implying that the ten laws Moses was given are, in fact, ten Universal Laws. The laws given were needed to correspond with the time and the circumstances in which he found himself. Those masses of humanity were so far askew that it was impossible to do anything more than to give them a few basics to restructure their society.

Some of the Commandments are not Universal Laws . . . you need to have a very clear understanding right at the outset of our work to know the difference between a Universal Law, a Contingent

Law, a Religious Law, and a Secular Law. The Commandments are filled with Contingent Laws—that is, laws created as a contingent to the environment and atmosphere of the time. Contingent Laws do not stand the test of time—nor do Religious or Secular Laws for that matter—but there is a subtle difference between them that must be explored. There is a purpose and a foundation of truth in every law, although many of them were conceived with ulterior motives attached. Universal Laws serve no one but the Creative Force and therefore have no ulterior motives. No one individual stands to profit by exploiting these laws—in other words, they favor no group, and certainly no cause. You won't find focus groups attached to them either. Their purity remains intact. The other laws, however, have less-than-pure motives at times, often written to accommodate a certain group or a certain issue.

If you like, you can write down the Ten Commandments for next time and we shall comment on each. We will spend the next few weeks exploring these laws so you have a clear understanding of each. As with all lessons shared in this Course, we shall not move on to the next one until it is clear to us that you have mastered the one before you. There is no Universal Law that begins "thou shalt not"—you shall see what we mean as we delve further into this topic. Theologians will be mortified, but your Creator will be pleased. This truly will be the road less traveled.

This missive confirmed what I had long believed, while simultaneously providing information I had never considered, specifically that laws fall into categories: a Universal Law, a Contingent Law, a Religious Law, and a Secular Law. This was new information—at least for me—and gave me pause to consider not only what it meant but where it was coming from. More importantly, was it true?

What struck me the most, however, was the statement, "There is no Universal Law that begins 'thou shalt not.'" As the words were being written, I felt a surge of energy signaling that this was an important message. Like most information coming from a soul writing session, this gem appeared toward the end. It was one of those "Truths" that permeates your senses.

I sat back in silence, pondering what it meant. It was true—I had never heard a Universal Law start with "thou shalt not." Universal Laws were not a set of demands. They had no "sin" attached to them. They were simple statements of truth, explaining to earthly students just how the Universe worked. You had a choice of living by them or ignoring them. It was a revelation to me, and I could not wait to begin the "course" that my Source would share over the next few weeks.

The following day I began the first of what would be many sessions discussing Universal Laws and the Ten Commandments. I realize that some of what was written may be controversial. My intent is not to debate these ideas, but rather to share the message exactly as it was written. If nothing else, it is certainly food for thought—ringing true for some and challenging others.

I began my meditation.

Commandment #1:

Thou Shalt Have No Other Gods before Me

When this was written, it was intended to dissuade the masses from glorifying manmade idols like the golden calf. The idea of worshipping a god is not contrary to Universal Laws as long as it does not blind a person to the Truth. Therefore, it is what the god represents that makes the difference.

As an example, Native Americans paid homage to all of Mother Nature, honoring the gifts the Creator bestowed on them—the sky, the earth, the trees, the animals, the water, etc. These were sacred

to them because they recognized them as coming from a protective source with the intent of providing them with food, clothing, and shelter. They honored these things in nature by not taking more than what they needed, by not abusing the gifts but learning to live harmoniously with them. While Christians viewed this as hedonistic, in fact it was as pure a form of worship as any civilization had come to understand. . . . By honoring nature and living alongside it in harmony, they touched the Divine. Therefore, they were closer to Center and more aligned with the Creator than the hordes of Christian conquerors who destroyed them as years went on.

In Moses's time, the people were in such a frenzied state that they would have worshipped anything they made which they deemed had monetary value. Out of this came greed and wantonness. They no longer saw the spirit of the Creative Force within each other—only the sensory attributes could satisfy their lust. They moved away from the harmony of the Universe into a place of earthy decadence. They were lost souls indeed. Few among them remained pure. Their frenzy was a contagion upon which each fed. It was only symptomatic of a greater degenerative direction humanity was heading into. Not a single Universal Law was remembered. Therefore, to get them to a starting place where minds could be reintroduced to the Universal Laws, the first of ten Contingent Laws was given—the one that ordered the dismantling of the golden calf and all other manmade symbols of worship.

While it is interesting to note that such idolatry continues to this day, few would recognize it as a part of the modern-day church. Yet what are statues but the images of human beings that are worshipped and prayed to? The tree in your backyard is more sacred than any statue. A blade of grass. A tiny insect. The gentle flowing waters of a creek. These are all symbols of the Creator, as they are all pure expressions of the Creative Force, which flows through all living things. Worshipping amid nature is more sacred than any church assembly. So many ancient civilizations knew this, yet built temples of glory to their designated deity—whether it be gods like Zeus or golden calves in Moses's time. These attempts at honoring the Creator were all dismal failures because they did not honor that which came from the Creator—they did not honor Life. They did not understand their place in the Universe. They did not attempt to live harmoniously with Nature and one another.

The Universe recognizes no "gods," and, as souls, you do not need to assemble such symbols to honor and worship in order to feel closer to the oneness of the Universe and the Creator. Place no one or anything before that connectedness. That is truly what that Law means.

Commandment #2:

Thou Shalt Not Make unto Thee Any Graven Images

This commandment is much like the first and as we have already commented on the issue of images, we do not feel additional input is necessary. In answer, however, to Karen's [my friend] question about the worship of man, since man is a part of the Creative Force as nature is—this is easily explained with a simple no. When men worship other men, they do so out of false reasons—generally because they believe these other men (or women) to be more powerful than they. They perceive of them as special, the chosen ones, who reached the pinnacle of their fame and fortune because they were above all others. The key word here is the word "more"—these kings and queens, movie stars, emperors and pharaohs, popes and bishops, millionaires or athletes give off an aura of "more than."

The Universe perceives all souls as equal. Did you not understand [in a past life] that the slave and master were equal in the eyes of the Creator, although to the master went all the honors, the titles, the fame, the adoration. These were earthly characteristics, not to be applied to the soul, for on that level it was the slave who made the most advances

in that life. Perception is a difficult thing to counteract, but you must always ask yourself: is this of the physical—again going back to the senses—or is it of the Divine? Can the physical be of the Divine? Yes, for is that not the whole purpose of your earthbound journey but to reach that state of oneness for body, mind, and soul? Few reach this level—those who have are no longer on the earth plane for they have evolved to the next level of evolution and ascended to a place where physical bodies do not exist. Who has created this hierarchy among humans except other humans?

Now you are thinking—there is a hierarchy among Divine Ambassadors, Guides, Angels, Oversouls, and other nonphysical beings who reside in the Etherland. This is not done as a way of judgment nor of adoration that one is elevated above the other. This is based on evolution, on levels of awareness, on experience, on assigned duty. It is a natural order, just as in nature there is what you call the food chain. Does this make the lion superior to the frog? No. In the Universe's makeup, each is equal, yet with different functions to perform and different assignments to undertake. A mighty oak tree may dwarf your beloved boxwoods, but that does not mean one is greater than the other. Each is true to its own nature and provides the beauty it was intended to provide—with no pretense, no jealousy, no "more than" attitude.

Which brings us back to the part in the commandment that says—"for I the Lord thy God am a jealous God, visiting the iniquity of the fathers upon the children unto the third and fourth generations of them that hate me. And showing mercy unto thousands of them that love me and keep my commandments." As you are aware, jealousy is a human emotion and like any human emotion cannot be applied to a nonhuman, most especially the Creator. Iniquities are not visited upon successive generations. Karma is the issue here, and Karma does not follow biological lines. It is attached to a soul who may have to deal with the issue of Karma in subsequent lifetimes in which that soul occupies a body that is not biologically connected to its previous incarnation. Seldom do souls reincarnate in the same biological family, although that is not to say it never happens. Your son in this life was your son in another; your daughter had been your mother. But these were in other biological families. You are not descendants of yourselves biologically, but you are descendants of yourselves on a soul level. Same soul over and over—just a different body.

The Universe does not show "mercy" nor does it mete out punishment, for those are not characteristics found in Universal concepts. You may believe mercy to be, but what is mercy but compassionate forgiveness. The Universe does not forgive because it does not blame. Accountability is done in the form of Karma—good or challenging. Each soul decides its own path—whether it creates a life where mercy is predominant or one in which it perceives of itself as being punished all the time. In either case, it is the earned Karma of that soul in play. No one is ever blamed or chastised or punished by a so-called righteous God. You are each your own righteous gods. Once souls are in between lives, they undergo a review and in this review are held accountable for their actions. This then translates to the life they create for their next incarnation. They may blame their woes on a vengeful, jealous God, but in fact, the one who orchestrates every lesson—whether painful or pleasant—is that soul itself.

We shall discuss Karma at long length when we get into Universal Laws, but hope all we have shared now suffices to address Commandment #2. We are with you always in love and in light.

Commandment #3:

Thou Shalt Not Take the Name of the Lord Thy God in Vain

Language is a human invention, for in the etheric realm, communication is not done in what you would call a verbal method. Within your language, you have decreed certain words as negative or positive depending upon the way they are used. To curse at the Creator, to show disrespect or anger, may not be an honorable thing to do from the human standpoint, but it changes nothing in terms of the way the soul must act out its incarnated destiny. To be angry, disrespectful, or have harmful, hateful thoughts toward anyone has dire consequences to the soul karmically, but it does not change the relationship between the soul and the Creator. When people use profanity, they are generally not attaching it to any deity in the first place. To say Goddamn someone does not mean they expect God to damn them. It is merely an expression of anger and outrage, a way to show displeasure toward another person, to not wish them well. Better the soul focus on what the underlying reason for the displeasure is than to worry about semantics. No loving creature wishes to be held in disdain. Therefore, profanities using God's name are hurtful simply because they show a lack of gratitude, understanding, and reciprocal love.

There was more to this message, but what I have quoted here gives you the gist of it.

Commandment #4:

Remember the Sabbath Day to Keep It Holy

Was the Universe created in six days and on the seventh day did the Creator actually rest? What need of rest does a nonphysical being have? The Universe does not operate in a linear field. Therefore, there is no such thing as passage of days because there is no time. Creation is instantaneous. The story of Creation in the Bible is pure fiction. The Creator did not say, today I shall create the sun, moon, and stars, and I'll get to the oceans tomorrow. In what you would call a blink of an eye, as quickly as a thought can be had, the Universe began, not in some orderly day-to-day fashion. The Creator, you know, did not operate from a Day Timer! We can discuss the creation of the Universe at another time. It is far too serious a topic to have it mentioned in the same breath—so to speak—as the fourth commandment which we can already see was predicated upon a misconception of how the Universe began.

The Creator, not existing in a linear place and time, does not designate one day over the next as holy, for all days are holy if on that day a soul connects to the All That Is. If you were to decide, for example, that each Tuesday you would go to a place that is sacred for you—whether that is a church, a temple, an altar in your yard, a bench in a park, a rock overlooking a river, or a stump in the forest— it does not matter. If you have deemed this place as sacred to you, it is because it has the energies that are aligned with your soul and enables you to feel closest to the Creator. So therefore if you designate Tuesday as being your day of connecting to the Creator and you honor it by the ritual of going to your sacred place and meditating so as to achieve that connection, then is not Tuesday a holy day for you?

We would say this Contingent Law was created to again acquire a sense of order in an otherwise frenzied and chaotic world. It was made to force everyone to go to a place together so they would be a captive audience for whichever messenger was on stage that week. It had merit, for some people did come to accept this as a holy day, a day which they spent in contemplation and in the company of those they loved. It is not a harmful law, except its message is riddled in guilt—another "you must do this or else" kind of gloom, doom warning. But it is not a law that applies to a Universal Law except by a very narrow definition. One could make an argument about what would be done on such a day to stretch it to fit Universal principles, but written as it is, it certainly is not in alignment with the laws the Creator set in place by which the entirety of the Universe operates. Don't forget—you are but one planet and one species. These laws were set down only for your planet. They don't exist elsewhere in the Universe, so that alone confirms that they cannot possibly be a Universal Law.

Commandment #5:

Honor Thy Father and Thy Mother

Finally, a commandment that does coincide with Universal Law because it centers on relationships between souls that involve Karma.

The relationship between parent and child is one of the strongest, most dynamic of relationships. Like all interactions with humans, there is much at play here. Souls are intertwined based on previous connections in former lives. This changes the dynamic of the relationship because the child may have been the parent before— or a sibling; a relative such as an aunt or uncle; a grandparent; or a friend, teacher, or lover. Souls do group together and reincarnate with the purpose of assisting each other in the lessons and growth opportunities presented to them. If it is deemed that a soul can best assist another by being the child or the parent, then the dynamic of that family is created.

With reversed roles come new challenges. Souls who were the parent before still run the dominant energy over the soul that was the child, even though their roles have reversed in their current incarnation. Your own daughter in this life runs that energy, as she was the mother in another incarnation. So not only must you deal with mother/daughter issues in this life, but you must temper that with the knowing that you are also dealing with the daughter/mother relationship from another life. Keeping in mind that we switch roles to augment the lessons presented is a very important parenting tool and when kept in the forefront of thought should lead to a greater respect between parent and child.

The other dynamic to keep in mind is that parents are chosen by their children, and not the other way around. Souls look at potential families and decide if that family has what is required to fulfill the purpose of its soon-to-begin life. It examines physical issues such as ethnic background and matches the appearance of the parents to what the intended appearance of the child will be. Physical features tend to remain the same from one life to another, even though race and cultural backgrounds may be different. The eyes always remain the same. It is true, they are mirrors of the soul, and, generally, experienced souls can recognize another just by searching for the identity in the eyes. Souls also examine potential parents in terms of environment, including financial situation, to coincide with issues concerning poverty or wealth they may be working on. They also consider talents, to coincide with whether they will be nurtured in whatever profession they are most suited for.

Yet to complicate matters, they also very closely examine attitudes and emotional/psychological makeup. This is most important above all others because it lays the very foundation upon which the soul will be challenged. Issues of abuse, alcoholism, drugs, gambling, indifference, etc., are important elements in the decision of whether that particular set of parents will best provide the environment the new soul requires to grow. Do not believe for a moment that souls choose only the wisest, most perfect physical and emotional specimens they can find. More often than not, they select parents whose own issues will cause them to be challenged deeply enough to overcome the deep-seated issues they themselves are struggling with. An alcoholic may choose to be born into an alcoholic family to learn the lessons of what his prior addiction did to his own children by being now the child of someone who drinks. A person who squandered wealth may return to a family steeped in poverty to understand and experience what it feels like to have nothing. And on it goes—it is the karmic dance.

Therefore, honor thy father and mother is a karmic law, for when all is considered, it is understood that the soul honored the souls of the parents by believing them to be most able to assist in its growth. That is an honor to be entrusted with the care and guidance of souls during their first years on the planet. Parents can gain much in their own karmic growth, depending on how they come to service that soul.

You may not agree with the choices your parents made nor feel comfortable in the relationship you have with them, but if you recognize they were playing out their own karmic dance, you can at least honor them for being souls who did what they could, given the circumstances of their own parental choices. In this way, you keep the fifth commandment and honor them in a way that is acknowledged in the Universe as one who sees and understands yet the greater picture.

Commandment #6:
Thou Shalt Not Kill

One might wonder what would account for the greater Karma. Does one transgression mean more than another? If you take a life, is the Karma more severe than if you deceive someone? The measure of karmic debt is made in regard to restitution. The eye for the eye philosophy in the Bible is akin to Universal Law in that it prescribes the paying back of that which was taken. This is justice in its truest form.

If a person commits murder in this life, does it stand to reason that he will be murdered in a future life? Not necessarily. If it is deemed that the cutting short of his life will be restitution enough, then that may occur, except that in doing so the cycle merely continues with the person who did the killing, now guilty and finding himself in a position of incurring the exact same Karma. However, circumstances could be thus that the person who incurred the karmic debt may lose a loved one to a senseless act of violence and have, as their karmic retribution, a lifetime of grief and loss to contend with—much as they caused the family of the person whose life was taken by them. Or there may be another way to repay the debt, such as a lifetime of being in service to prisoners like they were in a previous life. Or they may choose to return to life with a major disability. If a hand was raised, they may be born without hands or arms. So while it may not appear to be an eye for an eye in a literal sense, it is balanced in the end.

Thou Shalt Not Kill is not a Universal Law in the way it is written, but the concept is very much in line with Universal Laws.

Commandment #7:

Thou Shalt Not Commit Adultery

All five of the second five commandments are related to Universal Laws, primarily through the law of Karma. These are not written as Universal Laws—but they take in an ideology that is very much in keeping with Universal Laws. Therefore, we will not have much to say on these except to briefly tie in how they coincide.

On the subject of adultery. It may surprise you to learn that from a Universal perspective, monogamy is not necessary; that is, living one's entire life with one partner. People mistake lovers for soul mates and believe there is only one soul mate per soul. This is a fallacy, for soul mates merely means those souls with whom you have had a previous bond and who are with you again in this life to assist you. Consequently, friends are soul mates, as are children, parents, mates, and others close to you. However, there is only one Twin Flame, that mirrored soul that reflects you in their every breath. Twin Flames rarely incarnate together, preferring to avoid the distraction that they might cause one to the other. They each complement the other—so if there is a piece of you missing, the Twin Flame has it and vice versa. On occasion, Twin Flames do come together and join forces—giving twice the energy to an area in need of growth. But generally, people are romantically linked to soul mates.

As we said, there is more than one of these in your life. Therefore, it is ridiculous to think you could be attracted to only one mate. This is important to note. Whether you are monogamous or whether you have multiple mates is an individual decision. From the Universe's perspective, it is neither here nor there, except in one very important area, and that is in the case when the decision to seek another mate while still attached to another negatively impacts the soul of the

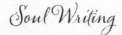

mate who is left behind. This is compounded by the pain caused to the children involved in that relationship. This is Karma of the highest nature. More ground is lost soul-wise because of adulterous relationships than any other so-called "sin." That is because it is done so frequently at such a high cost to others.

It is not always detrimental. At times the release of a spouse is actually very empowering and contains numerous and extremely valuable life growth lessons. If done in the proper way—and we know you are wondering how can it ever be proper—then no Karma is attached. Say one is in an abusive or loveless relationship, one that keeps them in torment and prevents them from fulfilling life's purpose. Along comes a soul who is a bright star, taking them by the hand, rekindling their spirit, showing them the power of love, regaining their self-esteem and confidence, and slowly pulling them out of that soul-threatening relationship. Then the soul has done a service to another—the person leaving to regain their soul, the person being left to reap the rewards of a manipulative, controlling, and self-absorbed life. It is a just exchange, including for children involved. But if no such circumstance exists, if the relationship is arbitrarily ended because of sins of the flesh, then there is a negative Karma accumulated and that must be accounted for.

We are not condoning adultery, nor are we condemning it. We do not view this action from a physical perspective—only from a soul perspective. Everyone sooner or later must account for every decision they make and are held accountable for these decisions. That is the way Karma works—and the measure by which all human actions are viewed.

Commandment #8:
Thou Shalt Not Steal

To take that which belongs to another is to deny your own self-worth. It is true that the Universe is an abundant source, which provides for all without thought of running dry. Therefore, if you believe in the Universal Law of Abundance, you would never give thought to taking from another. So it is if every soul came to understand and accept that there was enough set aside for just them, they would never take from another. Stealing occurs from fear—a fear of lack, of believing others have what you could never have unless you took it from them. Stealing is contrary to a Universal Law, which says that there is enough for each soul, therefore assuring that all your needs will be met. It may not be in the way you perceive it need be, but it is in the way that is for your highest and best. To refuse to accept that assurance and to take from others out of fear of lack is to defy the Universe and its wisdom. This is against many Universal Laws—not just one on abundance. It also defies the Law of Harmony, for it places you outside the harmonious sphere in which the Universe exists. Any time you stray from the path that remains in balance with the natural order of existence, you create disharmony, and that disturbance evolves into a negative Karma. When you stray from center, it requires a pendulum-like swing to return you to the harmonious path. Sometimes that pendulum must swing high into the opposite realm in order to have enough velocity to bring you back to center. As far right as you swing, that is how far left you must go to return to the middle ground that represents harmony. This is how all Karma works. The severity of the swing and its ramifications on one's life is dependent upon the Law of Grace—another Universal Law we shall eventually explore.

If you would but always remember that each of these laws is violated because of fear, you would come to understand why we say there are only two emotions—fear and love. If you operate from a place of love, there is nothing to fear. If you operate from a place of fear, there is no room for love. This is the ultimate lesson that all must learn. It is simplistic in its message, but it is true. Therefore, if stealing is a result of fear-based thoughts, does it not stand to reason that a heart filled with love would never consider taking from another? Love fills every crevice within a soul. There is no lack where love resides. Believe that especially at a time of perceived lack, for it is then that most gifts are lovingly bestowed upon you—the difference is in the perception.

Commandment #9:

Thou Shalt Not Bear False Witness against Thy Neighbor

Herein lies the heart of the Universal message—the issue of Truth. As a Truth Seeker, you are painfully aware of the heartache and suffering this commandment represents. Lives have been destroyed over false witness—and this has not lessened at all from the beginning of time. Children are as guilty of this as adults. It is the one Law that has been instilled in each heart, within each soul, yet it is the one Law that is so quickly forgotten and buried at the youngest of age. To bear false witness against a neighbor means more than the literal definition. Any falsehood is a testimony against someone or something. To lie about something is to lie about someone. One lie begets another and another and yet another. When one gets into the flow of such lies, it is impossible to escape. To bear false witness is against Universal Law not only because it creates the Karma of telling the lie that causes harm to another, but also because it is a direct violation of the Law of Truth.

Every soul made a solemn vow to be truthful in their experiences upon the Earth. It was believed that in so doing, souls could advance sooner because they would share with each other the true nature of the lesson they experienced. This would speed the process of evolution along, for it would mean only one soul need experience a lesson. The wisdom gained from that lesson would be passed on to the next soul. That soul would accept it as Truth because it was passed on by a Truth Seeker—one incapable of lying (for lies then did not exist). Why then would another soul respect that lesson? There would be no need because they would accept its Truth as their own and not have the desire or inclination to repeat it in any way. Imagine—by now your entire earthly experiences would have been long over and you would have all returned to Source having completed the salient lessons of the flesh as a collective group.

Unfortunately, those lessons of the flesh caused some souls to attempt to change the Truth to see if that would provide any advantage to them. It did in the short run, and that advantage was so huge that they began to believe it was better to alter Truth than to share it. Consequently, souls who were meant to learn lessons of the Truth were denied this and were instead introduced to lessons of falsehood. They were then doomed to repeat lessons on their own, no longer having the advantage of bypassing painful lessons by knowing of their Truth from another soul. They learned by falsehoods instead and that became their Truth.

And that is why you are all still here—and why the work of the Truth Seeker is so difficult. How do you combat centuries of lies? And to complicate matters, we now have those who call for "your own personal truth" which, as we said before, does not exist. There is only one Truth. You all know it. It has been imprinted on your souls. Truth Seekers remember. Others do not. They have layers and layers of falsehoods on their souls, which cause them continually to forget.

Until humanity remembers this Truth, it shall remain earthbound with only a handful of Truth Seekers ascending back to the All That Is. That is why this commandment as a Universal Law of Truth is so important to understand and express to others.

Commandment #10:

Thou Shalt Not Covet Thy Neighbor's House, Thou Shalt Not Covet Thy Neighbor's Wife, nor His Manservant, nor His Maidservant, nor His Ox, nor His Ass, nor Anything That Is Thy Neighbor's

This commandment is like the others in that it encapsulates the message brought forth from the previous Laws—that is, it is the same as stealing, adultery, and others that affect another soul's well being. Again, this commandment has to do with the Law of Abundance, in understanding there is an infinite amount of everything for each soul to use and to return. Therefore, it is never acceptable to take from another. It is taking from the Creator that which is not intended for you. We go back again to the Native American philosophy, which enabled them to live in complete and utter harmony. They took only that which they required to survive, and they gave back all that they took to ensure others of having a share in the abundance that nature provided.

This commandment is interpreted more as one of jealousy—of wanting what is another's, not so much in taking. But whether one lusts in their heart for that which is not theirs or takes it outright, the intention is what matters, and in this case, the intention is to take without any thought of giving back.

If you cut down a tree and do not replace it with another, have you not damaged the ecosystem of the forest? Have you not created a hole, a source of lack, a disharmony, or an imbalance? But if you take the tree, then plant another, are not all things then equal?

We are not saying that you can do this in all instances. You live in a very wasteful society where people are no longer self-sufficient but instead are dependent upon each other for their food and clothing and living supplies. It is more difficult to live in a harmonious world, balanced by the give-and-take philosophy of nature. Yet there are steps each soul can take to do their part in maintaining equilibrium.

To be desirous of what others have is to say you have no meaning nor value. It is a belief that some are arbitrarily blessed while others are left behind. You do not live in an arbitrary Universe. What may seem disproportionate is actually karmic in nature. It goes back to the savings-account theory. Those who seemingly have more have earned those things in prior lifetimes and are either cashing in on them now or pulling from their favorable karmic bank account. Those who lack may be working on lessons pertaining to lack or may be experiencing this perceived lack because of karmic debt. After all, lack is debt, is it not? And debt can be accrued in many ways—not merely in physical terms.

Therefore, do not look to what others have and compare to what you do not have and say—why don't I have these things and they do? Be assured there is a reason for all that exists within the Universe. You need to focus on what exists within your own home—that is, your own soul—and not on any others, for it is the promise of what you can accomplish that manifests in abundance, and this is always only dependent upon your actions. Remember, when a soul reflects on life that is over, it cannot use excuses or blame but only can defend that which he or she did while in the flesh. Think only unto yourself and eat the fruits of your own garden. It is sweeter by far than anything that exists beyond your own fence.

As with much of the information one receives from deep soul writing, its meaning remains dormant until the time is right for it to be recalled. This can happen weeks, months, or even years later. Something happens, and your mind retrieves that message, giving you one of those rare transformational moments.

Take Commandment #2, for instance: "Thou Shalt Not Make unto Thee Any Graven Images." Having grown up Catholic, I was accustomed to religious symbols being worshipped. Old churches had their share of statues, from Christ on the cross to Mary, Joseph, a host of angels, and saints. The priest would bow and the congregation would kneel before these images. When I was married in a Catholic ceremony, I was instructed to walk to the statue of the Blessed Virgin, present a bouquet of flowers at her altar, and pray to be a good wife and mother.

Thirty-two years later I accompanied my daughter and her fiancé to Wintergreen, Virginia, to look at a mountain site for their upcoming nuptials. As we stood at The Overlook, absorbing the awesome view of the mountains before us, I was struck by the silence—that same majestic silence one experiences at the Grand Canyon—and I told my daughter that this site was truly touched by God. Rather than worshipping materialistic images of the Almighty, I understood the impact of the words of that soul writing session nine years earlier, calling all of nature the "pure expressions of the Creative Force, which flows through all living things."

I spent several weeks exploring each of the Ten Commandments and their relationship to Universal Laws. This was the first time I followed a set curriculum, so in many ways, my writing sessions were the equivalent of attending a class each day. Throughout the "course," I was struck by the ways Spirit found to intertwine multiple lessons that I had not asked about but obviously was in need of knowing. Some of the messages were masterfully enlarged to address an ancient issue while simultaneously teaching a contemporary lesson. This was one of the few times that a complicated esoteric subject was addressed through my writing sessions. I did not expect that in a session talking about Universal Laws and the Ten Commandments that the material would expand to include topics attributing human emotions to a nonhuman entity, the concept of cellular memory and how it relates to understanding karmic law, and theories of reincarnation.

During this particular session, occasionally I experienced a different energy coming in to explain a lesson—as if a substitute teacher had entered the classroom. The teacher who commented on the ineffective use of a verbal language versus a seemingly undisclosed, nonverbal language that we had not mastered yet was a new voice among my Muses.

Sometimes I would access a teacher who exuded a sense of humor in comments, as with the messenger who said, "The Creator, you know, did not operate from a Day Timer!" Interesting how this opened a dialogue about time and time travel. I was reminded that the Universe does not operate in a linear field, and therefore one could not measure the passage of time in a plane of timeless existence. In effect, this challenged the biblical notion that the Universe was created in "six" days.

The other point well made was the human tendency to use guilt to motivate behavior. The "you must do this or else" sentiment expressed in any of the Commandments is in stark contrast to Universal Laws that are simply statements of how a harmonious Universe works. In Universal Laws, Karma, as opposed to sin, is the motivating factor.

In "Honor Thy Father and Mother," my writings explored the complicated relationship between parents and children from a physical, spiritual, and metaphysical perspective. Some of the information was a confirmation of what I already knew—that children choose their parents to experience growth opportunities that are most likely to occur within the dynamic of that particular family structure. The message here is not so much that one should honor one's parents simply because they are your parents but because you chose them. They are honoring you by providing a family structure in which you can learn and grow while working out karmic issues. Looking at parents from this perspective creates a new avenue from which to review the relationship. Often that perspective encourages healing because it acknowledges the role each family member plays in each other's soul development. This writing session enabled me to reexamine the dynamics between my parents and me, and between my children and me.

Exploring "Thou Shalt Not Kill" brought up the meaning of justice—in this case, karmic justice, or cause and effect. My writings gave me a detailed lesson on how Karma works. Payback—or a return to the center wherein harmony exists—is inevitable, no matter what the crime. The method exacted for such payback is not doled out by a karmic supreme court, but by the soul itself in such a way as to experience and understand the gravity of the transgression. The idea of a balanced Universe is repeated in Universal Laws. If one goes too far in one direction, circumstances will arise to create equilibrium and bring the soul back to center. Every act—good, bad, or indifferent—has a consequence. At one time or another, that consequence will manifest. Therefore, the message of this soul writing session was intended to draw the reader away from a specific act—for example, taking a life—and instead focus on the ways in which karmic justice unfolds. When stated as such, it is clear that Karma is by far a much more demanding philosophy to live by than sin.

Interesting to note that in the discussion about adultery, this "sin" was viewed less as a moral dilemma and more as a growth issue, making it further askew from having religious consequences. Initially it surprised me to learn that, "From a Universal perspective, monogamy is not necessary." After some thought, it was understandable how this could be the case.

The value of this particular message, however, was in the clarification of the difference between soul mates and Twin Flames. I often hear people mistakenly believe that they have only one soul mate and that the person is always a love interest. They believe having a soul mate in one's life supersedes any other relationships. This message reiterated that one has many soul mates and that they are not confined to love interests.

The last writing session on "Thou Shalt Not Steal" was interesting in that not one but three Universal Laws are mentioned—the Law of Abundance, the Law of Harmony, and the Law of Grace. In doing so, Spirit was connecting the dots, so to speak, between each of the laws. One impacts another, which impacts another, which impacts another. The Universal connection of all things is outlined in this passage. So is the premise of *A Course in Miracles*—that there are only two emotions—fear and love. This, as my Source writes, is the "ultimate lesson that all must learn."

What strikes me the most about each commentary on the Commandments is that the message is not so much about not doing something, but that by showing a different perspective, you come to the conclusion of *why* do it at all? In the case of "Thou Shalt Not Steal," we are reminded, "The Universe is an abundant source which provides for all without thought of running dry. Therefore, if you believe in the Universal Law of Abundance, you would never give thought to taking from another."

Through soul writing, I learned this simplistic yet powerful philosophy was the difference between a Commandment and a Universal Law. If you truly understand the karmic ramifications of perpetuating any action that is not in harmony with the Universe, then that is the greatest deterrent of all. It would not be easily dismissed in the confessional. It would be a permanent mark in your karmic register, and sooner or later, you would have to erase that mark either through the Law of Grace or through karmic retribution.

In my brief exploration of religious philosophies through soul writing, I learned that Universal Laws are more difficult to live by than the Ten Commandments because they are inescapable. There are no loopholes. No get out of jail free cards. No unimpeded advancement to GO with an extra two hundred dollars in your pocket. Yet for souls yearning for justice, living by karmic law is the only way to make sense out of living in an unjust world. *That* is the difference and, based on the lessons learned in this several-week course, one well worth knowing.

CHAPTER NINE

Soul Writing for Guidance on Specific Topics

Many writers use deep soul writing to answer specific questions. They write out the question and wait for guidance. Some engage in a conversation with questions posed and answers received. I seldom did this, preferring to just check in and see what my higher self thought was important for me to know on that particular day. I usually did not know in advance what would be presented and almost always there was some nugget in the middle of the missive that had nothing to do with anything I was thinking about at the time. Early on I saw a pattern in which the writings could be categorized. I considered the benefit of this form of stream-of-consciousness guidance. Rereading months of correspondence, I began to pull out portions of the copy, assign it to a topic category, and thus create my own encyclopedia of transpersonal definitions. It should be noted that these messages came early in my soul writing experience, and while the specific issues I was dealing with are no longer applicable, the guidance, nonetheless, is universal and stands the test of time. Here's an A–Z sampling of the myriad subjects that were addressed in those early days.

Accepting Help

Ask for help and then accept it in whatever way it comes. Do not be afraid to say what you want—just say it.

Advice (on Giving)

We cannot, are not allowed, to instruct you on what to do. That is for you to decide. We are here to guide, to give comfort.

All Answers Lie Within

We are aware of your need to have answers, and while we may not provide the concrete responses you so earnestly request, we would say to you that again you need not inquire outside yourself for answers to questions that arise from your very soul, for who can answer these but.you. . . .

Aloneness

The Visionary's road is lonely. It is all right to feel that way; yet always remember, even in the midst of your despair, that you are not alone, not now, not ever. Spark the fire. Be a catalyst for positive change. Touch their hearts and their souls, as only you are able. And if on your journey you come to the realization that you must go alone, then go forward bravely. You will be rewarded in the end.

Animal Totems

Your symbol of the gentle deer is a powerful totem. It was sent to give you strength, to go forward, to let go; for what is ahead is much more meaningful than what is now. The fawn will lead you through all fear, all strife. She will guide your way to a calm, peaceful center that will lift you out of the chaos and turbulence that surrounds you. She reminds you of the gentleness of spirit, the serenity that is within your soul. She was alone on the road in an environment that was foreign to her, threatening to her, dangerous to her, but she bravely went forward to seek you out; for her mission was for you and only you, and she risked all to fulfill that mission. So it is with you, dear child, alone on your path in a world that is foreign to you, threatening to you, dangerous to you. Yet you, like the fawn, have a mission to seek out others. In your case, you must seek out the souls of all who need you to give them a message, a safe passage through the dark forest of their lives. Your light will lead the way.

Balance

Work today on getting the most from your day. Waste no time, for time is precious when you consider all you need to accomplish in such a short time. Balance, little one; that is equally important. Work hard, but set aside time for fun. Give yourself a well-deserved treat from time to time. You deserve it. You are a child of God.

Balance and Retribution

You are safe because you are loved and because you are a part of a greater whole. To pick away at you is to pick away from the Totality—thus the lesson that whatever is done to the one is done to the whole. Allow your Creator to work in maintaining balance. Should a soul stray too far from center, it will encounter situations and circumstances to bring it back in line.

The Beginning

At the dawn of time when all souls were one, there was an agreement made to create a place where the senses could experience all the emotion, all the physical realities that did not exist in Spirit.

But with the physical came all the issues that were unforeseen by those in Spirit. Once caught up in the issues that exist only on the Earth, there was a great desire to return to Spirit, but the way back was not as simple as the way to the Earth, for now it was time to unlearn all that came with being in the physical body and that was a sizable undertaking, one that is still being learned today. Yet in that learning is the light that shows the way home, and it is that path that all must follow, each in his or her own way and in his or her own time.

Centered and Focused

Take a deep breath, keep asking for guidance, for it is there for the asking. Then move forward calmly. Allow the chaos of the exterior world to go around you and not touch you. Stay centered and focused. Should you falter and lose sight of your path, we will illuminate the way. The light around you is indeed very bright. Let it shine for others—a beacon for others to follow.

Despair

You are growing weary, are you not? We see you fighting to stay in the moment. Do not despair. We are with you. You are not alone. It is growing more difficult; we know this. You are feeling more and more defeated. You wonder why you should even continue. We understand and do not judge you for these feelings. It seems to you there is no way out, but it only appears that way; there is a way out, and it is lurking close at hand. You will figure out a way; do not doubt your ability to do so. Whatever your decision, it will be the right one. You have not come all this way just to fail. What would that serve? Seek counsel wisely. Then be still. Above all, have no fear. And rest.

Ego

We understand your human condition that compels you to fluctuate from ego to higher self in a continual battle for control. At times you give in to ego, and how does that feel? Fearful, painful, anxious, is it not? Yet when you come from higher self, how do you feel? Peaceful, joyful, calm, and happy, are you not? You are on the Earth to learn balance and to learn to love, and you cannot do either coming from the ego.

Fear

Focus more on moving away from the energies that have held you back. There are so many options you have refused to follow. Why? Fear. Fear of rejection. Fear you won't do it right. Fear of not being loved or accepted. Self-conscious fear, no? We tell you, fear does not exist. None of that is true. So why put any unnecessary energy into it any longer when all it does is hold you back? The Holy Spirit perceives your fear as saying you really don't want this and therefore, as it only will give you what you do want, will not grant your desire to move. Eliminate the fear and you remove the block, and thus your wish will be granted.

Freedom

What earthly bonds can enslave you when in God's eyes you are as He? Is God a slave? Is He in bondage? So how can you be either?

Fulfillment

You have begun the process of remembering who you truly are, and with that remembrance comes a power and a strength that will lead you through the coming days with a clear focus and a willing heart. Keep going. You are in the hands of the Universe who loves you greatly and who wishes for you only the fulfillment of your soul's deepest desire, which is to be one with the Creator. Using your creative abilities will do that for you, for in tapping into that power within you and using it to positively affect others, you will do your Father's work and be rewarded accordingly. Of that, have no doubt. And do think on this. To do your Father's work is the ultimate goal of each soul. What is there to fear in fulfillment? There is only joy and peace.

Issue Resolution

You are not of this world, yet you live in this world, and while you are here, you must work through each issue you brought forward until it is resolved, and you are free to move on. You have been examining these issues with a true awareness of self. Few take the time to examine themselves in such minute detail as you. No one can offer criticism of you that you have not already given to yourself. We would say, rather than be critical, which implies you are less than perfect, why not recognize that you are not the issues you apply to yourself? They are separate and outside of you. They are not serious, just minor fine tunings.

Joining (The Power of Three)

Three is the most powerful combination. When three minds join as one, they become the Master Mind, and thoughts that emanate from that energy are enormous in power and influence. It is as close to perfection as you can achieve in physical form.

Karma

You are aware that the actions of the past are directly related to the actions of today. This is the law of balance and harmony. Many of the talents and abilities you have brought with you into this life are those you cultivated before. You have always been a writer, a teacher, a philosopher, a theologian, a musician, and an artist. You have been many things to many people.

Letting Go

Now is the time to make a tremendous leap forward as you discard the many distractions you have created for yourself in the past. As you release and let go, you allow the universal life energy to rush in and fill you with the commitment and sense of purpose that lies ahead.

Life Lessons

The lemons you are dealing with now are indeed very sour. It will take a lot of sugar on your part to sweeten this pot. So pour it in, and then and only then can you sit back, put your feet up, feel the breeze on a porch that is not yet yours, and sip the cool, sweet, refreshing taste of the most exquisite lemonade ever created on the planet Earth!

Love

Love never dies. It never waivers. It never deceives. It is the truest essence of spirituality. It survives when all else is lost.

Meditation

Now is the time for action, yet this also is the time for quiet contemplation. How to do both simultaneously, you ask? We would say to you that quiet contemplation is action. It is the act of going inside for the answers to your questions rather than remaining stagnant and doing nothing. Quiet contemplation is not doing "nothing." It is very much an activity unto itself. In closing your eyes and quieting your mind, the voice of Guidance can be heard, and if heard, can motivate and inspire you to action.

Movement of Time

You wonder about time. You feel it passes too slowly when it comes to you getting on with your life's work. It passes as it needs to, in a natural progression, one step at a time, no step taken before its time. How quickly it happens is up to you, for you and only you know what needs to be done. If you do not do it, time slows for you, ever patiently waiting for you to catch up. Yet when you do what needs to be done, time cooperates, and you move forward rapidly. It is all very natural.

Past Lives

Each of you has an ability and a talent that is particular to your life force energy. . . . Tap into that infinite power within you, for nothing has been lost over all these centuries. Every ability you have ever perfected, every skill you have acquired, every ounce of knowledge you have absorbed—all of this is still yours. Every good deed you performed, every time you thought of others instead of yourself, every time your discoveries helped thousands of others, all of these things were put in your "universal bank account" for you to draw upon at some future date.

Peace

You remember the peace and blissfulness of Spirit and how you long to be there. Yet for you the reason you are on the Earth plane now is to attain that same level of peace and blissfulness in a physical body as you did in a spiritual body. Impossible, you say? It is not impossible for those who achieve that level of awareness that allows them to transcend the bonds of earthly existence and go beyond such to achieve a state of surrender that ultimately produces a happiness from within that cannot be usurped by anything—any person, thought, place, or thing—in bodily form.

Present Moment

Remember each dream is but a reflection of the deepest desire of your soul; each wakeful memory is but a reminder of what will be, not what was. The past and the future do not really matter. One is over; the other has not begun. The present is all that is real. The present you have created is the culmination of the work you have done in the past; the future will be the culmination of all you do in the present.

Protection

If you can but find a way to put a shield around you, to be immune to the negativity that is constantly bombarding you, then you will be able to go forward untouched by any of the multitude of false prophets who show up at your door seeking to weaken your resolve so their own irresponsible acts would be justified and made stronger.

Soul's Purpose

You know deep within what you want. You know deep within how to acquire it. Whenever you do something, ask yourself: is this part of my soul's purpose? Will this ultimately help me to fulfill my destiny? If the answer is no, then let it go. You cannot afford to hold on to anything that keeps you from fulfilling your destiny, and yet most of what you have done thus far has done just that. Until now it has been because you are fearful or felt unworthy or did not believe it possible. Now you are awakening to who you really are, and when you fully awaken, then you will no longer have any fear nor feelings of unworthiness. You will believe it is possible because it will unfold as you envision it to be.

Spirit Guides

In the physical, one falls asleep and forgets who they are. We merely serve as a constant alarm clock, one that refuses to turn off until we are certain you are truly awake. . . . Know that the Universe, in its love for you, would not do anything to hurt you or lead you astray. Our purpose in guidance is to offer you options, alternative modes of thinking, to present you with another picture, a way for you to understand the bigger picture and stay centered and focused on your goals.

Synchronicity

There are no accidents, no coincidences. Everything is happening as planned, but only because one is wise in seeing opportunities for what they are and then following one's intuitive sense about manifesting them at the proper hour. Do not rush the process. In your caution—and most of all, your trust—you work cooperatively with the Universe and so it unfolds as planned. . . . Your pattern is one of accidental discovery. You always "stumble" onto something when you are least thinking of it. It just "happens." In truth, you did all the preliminary work yourself. When you reach a certain point, help from our side becomes manifest, and suddenly something "unfolds" before your very eyes. It seems like an accident to you, but it is not an accident at all. After all, there are no accidents, no coincidences. These "accidental discoveries" are always monumental, and they are always to help others, to benefit large numbers of people, not just a handful.

Trust

Go forward knowing that the Universe loves you, is supporting you, is fulfilling your every wish and desire in ways you are unaware of. If you will just maintain your belief, that is all we ask. Keep believing, even when it is easier to despair; even when it looks as though everything is lost, that it no longer exists, it is still there. The tests just grow more difficult as you get closer to the goal, but it is not anything you cannot rise above. It is only to strengthen you, to prepare you for the road ahead.

Truth

The most important lesson is to stand for truth and honesty and nothing else. There is no guilt in truth. There is no fear in truth. There is only oneness with the Creator. Your task is as all others, to speak truth, to live truth, to be the embodiment of truth. You live in a less-than-honest world, but you come from a Source that is only truth, so it is that Source you will return to. It is that Source you are a part of now.

CHAPTER TEN

Soul Writing as a Tool for Psychoanalysis and Healing

Writing—like talking—has a cathartic quality to it. But unlike talking, soul writing produces deeper levels of insight. Going within and trusting the Source of the writing can lead to understanding the profound meaning of issues one is experiencing. Writing is a form of self-expression, and soul writing is the self-expression of the soul, providing a safe place for individuals to explore Truth. Doing so often results in a shift in perspective, and that, in and of itself, can be a powerful tool for healing.

In *Opening Up: The Healing Power of Expressing Emotions,* James W. Pennebaker, PhD, wrote about a period in his life in which he was unable to cope with depression. He began a daily ritual of writing, during which he expressed his feelings and thoughts about every aspect of his life, from his marriage to his parents to his career. While he admits to feeling exhausted after these sessions, he said he began to feel freer. Within a week, he noticed that his depression had lessened, and he sensed a new meaning and direction in his life. Looking back on this time, he recognized that it was the writing that helped him let go and work through a number of personal issues, providing psychological and physical benefits to his life.

Today writers are going into health institutions to teach a form of soul writing to patients suffering from catastrophic illness, such as cancer. Through deep soul writing, patients are able to express their emotional reaction to their illness: how it is affecting their families; their fears; and, more importantly, their connection to a Higher Source for comfort, understanding, and hope.

But terminally ill patients are not the only ones who can benefit from learning how to write from the deepest part of their being. People who deal with stress on a daily basis, those who suffer from anxiety attacks, and those dealing with depression or other emotional upheavals can benefit from establishing a regular date to do soul writing. New mothers can use it to express their frustrations. Seniors can use it to reflect on their lives. Teens can use it to examine their insecurities. Divorcees can use it to vent their feelings of abandonment and isolation—or their exhilaration of being free from a stifling and painful relationship. Widowers can use it to work through their grief.

While soul writing does much to alleviate the anxiety attached to these conditions, it is not a cure-all for life's major challenges. It does, however, give you insights to enable you to better understand your feelings. It creates an objective platform that puts some distance between you and what's going on in your life so that you can view it from another perspective.

Anyone who has seriously pursued soul writing ov
long period of time will tell you that the information gained
provides valuable insights about life. Issues you struggle with
in a conscious state are often easily explained when writing
in an altered state; so much so that the writer is surprised
they did not come to the revealed conclusion independently.

This often happens to me. My mind is troubled by something, and despite my best efforts to psychoanalyze myself,
the origin of the problem and its ultimate solution does not
reveal itself. Through the process of soul writing, suggestions come forth that lead to a satisfactory resolution or, at
the very least, a different angle that previously had not been
considered.

Formulating the right question can be the hardest part of
doing soul writing for analyzing one's issues and challenges.
This requires a degree of honesty that some find painful; yet
to understand the root cause of a problem, those kinds of
uncomfortable questions must be asked.

When you are facing an emotionally draining condition,
take out your pen, meditate, and then ask: For what purpose
have I brought this situation to me? What lesson is there in
my having to deal with this issue? Why do I need to learn this?
What about it is symptomatic of a larger problem? When did
this issue begin? What triggered it again and why? What role
does the person bringing this lesson to me have to play in my
life? How can I come to a place of forgiveness and healing?
How can I best interact with this person for our greater good?

Using soul writing to ask questions pertaining to personal
issues can point to something that had not entered your
consciousness. Say you are having marital problems and you
question why you chose your partner in the first place. What
unseen factors played a role in that choice? Was it a karmic
connection, and, if so, what was the origin of the problem

that plagues the relationship now, and how can you resolve it for the benefit of both parties? What lesson does your partner bring to the relationship, and, similarly, what lesson are you providing your partner? What is the purpose of your union? Who else is affected by your relationship and why?

Answers to these questions will provide insights to help you better understand the dynamics of your relationship. Once you are enlightened to the unseen causes of the issues that bubbled to the surface through this relationship, you can proceed without the kind of regret that comes from making hasty decisions without knowing all the facts.

This method of asking for and receiving divine guidance through soul writing can be applied to all areas of your life, including relationships with family members, friends, business colleagues, neighbors, church members, etc. Knowing the *why* of something helps to understand the *how* of something else. "I feel this way because . . ." Once known, you can step back and take a more objective look at the situation. Often, knowing it is a learning opportunity enables us to feel gratitude rather than resentment. It sprinkles a little sugar on an otherwise sour experience. You come to see the bigger picture and realize that for every feeling you have and issue you face, there is an answer available through deep soul writing. You simply have to make the commitment to explore it.

This being said, it is worth noting that while the use of soul writing as a method of soul searching is considered normal and acceptable to proponents of transpersonal studies, there are still mainstream medical and mental health professionals who are likely to challenge it. Reviewing it from a scientific perspective rather than a spiritual perspective, these researchers have determined that information obtained through guided writing is more often than not the musings of someone suffering from a dissociative disorder rather than someone who has found a way to communicate with a higher power. It is often easier for mainstream professionals—who know no other way than what their traditional education has taught them—to put someone exhibiting unexplained phenomena in a box with a label on it than it is to accept that divine forces are at play.

As can be expected, psychiatrists dealing with a patient who is adept at guided writing begin to dissect the patient's personality, looking for clues to explain the source of what they deem to be abnormal behavior.

This was especially prevalent in the early twentieth century, when automatic writing was all the rage. In the late 1920s, Dr. Anita M. Mühl did extensive research on patients who exhibited what she identified as "automatic writing." She used automatic writing to discover what was going on in the minds of her patients, which she was unable to access with ordinary questioning. In doing so, she focused on how writing could be used as a tool to successfully psychoanalyze individuals exhibiting a wide array of psychotic tendencies.

Despite the fact that her research was done nearly one hundred years ago, it nonetheless came to the same conclusions as those drawn by many contemporary psychoanalysts, who believe that if a person's mental health is weakened through an unpleasant experience or idea, then a secondary personality forms and operates independently—usually without the knowledge of the primary personality. Mühl believed it was this secondary personality that produced the writing in an unconscious attempt to find answers to the issues facing the writer. Therefore, she concluded that individuals who exhibited a well-defined dissociative personality were more suited to doing guided writing than those who did not.

This is untrue, especially when applied to soul writing. Nearly everyone who tries soul writing is successful on his or her first attempt. Further, research has shown that individuals on medication or those suffering from any form of psychosis are less likely to be successful candidates for entering an altered state of consciousness—the same state required to do soul writing.

Despite her predisposition to the psychological explanation of automatic writing, Mühl admitted that some of the material produced using this method of communication was, in her own words, "simply amazing." Her research showed that individuals engaging in guided writing began exhibiting talents unknown to them in a conscious state—such as the ability to compose music; to write poetry or stories; to illustrate or design; or an increased aptitude in math, history, geography, or foreign languages.

As a scientist, however, Dr. Mühl distanced herself from the spiritual side of guided writing. In doing so, she, like others who view only the scientific side of this work, failed to see that this form of writing has the potential to lift a person's soul to find answers to life's many questions through divine guidance.

The concept of inspirational writing, as outlined by Edgar Cayce, was not known at this time, so it may be unfair to make the comparison of what Mühl labeled as "automatic writing" with what Cayce said about the difference between the two. However, it is interesting to note that Mühl foreshadows Cayce's concerns about the use of automatic writing as an open invitation to possession by lesser-evolved spirits.

Inspirational writing uses prayer as a means of safeguarding the individual from these dangers. Consequently, any messages received in this manner give the writer a sense of being a part of a greater whole. Soul writers accept responsibility for what appears on paper, viewing the messages as loving and enlightened messages from a Higher Source.

Mühl admitted that guided writing was a valuable means of studying unconscious trends and motives and of discovering latent abilities, but she cautioned that it could also be a dangerous tool in the hands of an unscrupulous or untrained individual. There is truth in this idea. Like any misused or misunderstood gift, guided writing can do great damage if it comes through a soul who has ulterior motives for its use. Those who are not grounded or sincere can use it to mislead others through exploitive psychic readings or channeling sessions. These individuals can pretend to be in touch with the Source of good, yet without proper safeguards can inadvertently allow lesser spirits to dictate messages that have no basis in divine guidance.

Luckily, today guided writing is much more than a trendy parlor game. It is not unusual to see it being used by reputable psychologists who have incorporated it into their clinics and labs as a viable tool for contacting the subconscious.

For those who have the highest ideal and purest intent, soul writing is a means of expressing those unacknowledged ideas of the higher self and for that reason is a valuable tool in the spiritual schoolbag of every soul.

CHAPTER ELEVEN

Writing for Soul's Growth

One of the reasons I prefer to use the term "soul writing" is because it so aptly describes the highest form of service this tool of transformation provides. In all the years and all the ways I have used inspirational writing, the one area where it has consistently provided invaluable guidance is in matters addressing my soul's growth. I have come to rely on this divine gift whenever I am seeking a different perspective on my life, to get unstuck when I am mired in problems, to grab onto it as a life preserver when I feel as though I am sinking. The process never gets old, and the information always gives me insights I am certain I would not get from writing in a conscious state.

It is my belief that everything we do is intended as a means to learn lessons that resolve Karma and free our souls to move through this school we call Earth until we have had the opportunity to explore all manner of physical, emotional, mental, and spiritual experiences. That is, after all, why we incarnated in the first place—to accumulate wisdom through earthly experiences.

There is much to learn while in physical form, but those lessons have the most meaning when placed in the context of the soul's experience. The journey from the physical plane to the spiritual one is long, and, depending on the curriculum we choose, it can be wrought with passages that seem unnavigable. In human existence, the question of "why" is most often asked as a means of finding reason in an oftentimes unreasonable world. *Why* can't I find love? *Why* do I have to deal with this illness? *Why* am I so unhappy? *Why* am I struggling financially? The endless search for the answer to *why* can be found in soul writing.

When put to the question in inspired writing, the answer reveals itself, and it is that answer that illuminates the way from *why* to *I see*. Once the darkened path becomes enlightened and the answer to the *why* question is clear, then the issue surrounding the question is resolved and put to rest. By putting it behind you, you are able to move forward to the next lesson. Each question-and-answer session is a step upon a ladder. You ask. Spirit answers. One step up. To do this on a regular basis assures you of constant movement. A soul that seeks answers from the Divine Source does not remain stagnant. It is constantly inching upward, closer and closer to the Source from which it came.

Words are powerful tools. When presented in a particular voice—a voice familiar to a soul that draws comfort from its guidance—it creates a shift in consciousness. When you are in a meditative state, you are so close to God that you ascend to a higher level of consciousness. A sense of peaceful coexistence permeates every part of your being, and you are in such a blissful state that you are lifted away from the problems and unpleasantness that surround you. You turn your attention to solutions and focus on the beauty of a Universe that remains perfect in every way despite the chaos that may exist on this physical plane.

When you are in alignment with that energy and initiate an exchange with divine thought through inspired writing, you are elevated to a different place in time. You sense a universal balance and harmony. It is in that moment that the soul expands to take in the wisdom of the Creative Forces. It sees as it was meant to see. It hears as it was meant to hear. It feels as it was meant to feel. It senses an expanding awareness, and it grows to envelope that awareness. It asks the questions. It embraces the answers. It is an endless ebb and flow of inspired thought, of expansive vision, of perfection of the senses to achieve heights not possible in a conscious state.

The soul engages in this dance through the pen, and the wisdom it shares with the collective unconscious is without limits. Soul writing enables you to leave your earthly confines and soar to unbelievable heights. It fulfills the promise of "ask and ye shall receive." But remember, you must *ask* the question first, expressing a sincere desire for assistance. Souls are naturally curious, trying to remember their place of origin and how to return there, while still accomplishing what they set out to do on this side of the veil. It is natural to raise questions about the Universe while contemplating it from a physical body on planet Earth. In Spirit, there are all the answers to all the questions. To travel from the place of only questions to the place of only answers, one must learn to let go and be lifted from one to the other by simply asking the question and listening for the answer.

It is something that can be done in meditation for certain, but how often after a meditation do you actually remember the answer that Spirit provided? In soul writing, the answers appear on a page for you to revisit. There is no misunderstanding, no reading between the lines, no need for curious interpretation that could be misconstrued. Instead, you receive an honest, straightforward response. Rereading it only strengthens its meaning—a meaning that is fluid and changes as time evolves and you evolve. The truth of the message remains the same, but as you grow, you absorb its message in a deeper way.

A soul that thus engages in a continual conversation with the Divine grows in the wisdom imparted, and over time the messages present novel ideas and creative expressions that spiral higher and higher until the soul and the Source are united once again.

Here is an example of the kind of guidance I receive through soul writing. Several years ago, I was thinking about making a change in my writing career. I was trying to get the courage to focus more on inspirational writing and less on the features I write for local magazines. This would have meant a loss of income and hence my fear about making that change. Meditating on that thought, I received the following guidance:

My dear child, we are with you always in love and in light. Stay true to whom you are. How long have you taken the road most traveled? You have sought a place in a world that is not you. How much more at peace would you be if you understood your role and believed in who you are and in all who invisibly surround you to give you all the love, nurturing, and guidance you so desperately long for? Of late you have reviewed the choices you have made that took you away from your work and so clearly showed you the pattern that these choices resulted in—always taking you farther from your authentic self and from the work you are here to do. How many times have you experienced the elation of using the gifts you have been given for the betterment of self and others?

Now is the time to transition from doing the bidding of others to finally doing the bidding of your Creator who breathed into your soul the gift of inspiration. You may not see yourself so clearly in this role and it is understandable, for your life has not been one in which you have drawn to yourself the inspiration to model after. Instead, you have encountered many obstacles to keep you from touching the inspired place within you, except on too rare an occasion. Yet what is it your soul longs for but the freedom that can only be expressed in the written word? Fear not. You believe you are not courageous—that the time for you has passed—but it is not so. Time knows no passage for a soul who is eternal. It is only the continuance of work begun long ago. Separate yourself from the negative thoughts, for they are not you. Do not say, "no, I cannot" but instead embrace life, saying, "yes I can."

Remember always your divine birthright—remember always you are not alone, although at times it feels as though you are. All of nature is with you, surrounding you. The beauty that is music, the comfort of the wind upon your face, the sweet smells of the flora, the affection of animals—the sun in the sky, the soft sound of rain—are all yours. Remember that you are never, never alone. We leave you in love and light.

I opened my eyes with a sense of peace and gratitude. The same feeling is available to anyone who uses this wonderful gift for guidance in his or her life. Soul writing expands one's awareness, for it is the pure and uncensored voice of the soul.

CHAPTER TWELVE

The Soul Writing Research Project

As I came close to completing my studies at Atlantic University, I had one major assignment to tackle before earning my degree. It wasn't hard for me to select a topic for my "culminating project." My decades of experience, coupled with the depth of information on the creative process coming out of my course work at A.U., made inspirational writing the ideal choice. Here, I use the term "inspirational" writing rather than "soul" writing in keeping with the terminology Edgar Cayce used in his readings.

Once the faculty approved my subject, I designed the project to be both service related and creative. My goal was simple. I would teach the writing process to a group of volunteers and then lead them through a series of exercises to explore the various ways inspirational writing could be applied to their lives. I designed each session around a different topic, giving the group an opportunity to experience how inspirational writing can be used to address various issues. With each session, they deepened their ability to connect to Source for guidance. My hope was that they would view inspirational writing as a means to enrich and better their lives. This was the service portion.

A secondary intent was to compile the results of the study, intermix it with my own experiences, and chronicle both for future publication in this book. This was the creative portion.

I began in March 2009 by conducting a free lecture on inspirational writing for A.R.E. members and guests in the Charlottesville, Virginia, area. Afterward, I invited the audience to become a part of my research group; from this pool, I gathered volunteers who were willing to commit to the five-month writing portion of the project.

For the purpose of deciphering the demographic of the group and to determine their level of experience with altered states of consciousness, I developed a questionnaire for each volunteer to complete. This helped determine a common starting point.

Eight participants—all female—made up my research group. They ranged in age from fifty to seventy-seven, with the majority (six) in their fifties. For the purpose of the project's report and this book, they gave me written permission to refer to them by first name.

Five of the eight stated they did not feel proficient in entering or exiting a meditative state or altered state of consciousness. However, they all said they had been in a state of inspiration where ideas just began to manifest.

Of the eight, three had never heard of inspirational writing before, but all were familiar with the term "automatic writing." Four indicated they did not know the difference between the two, and three stated they had never done either before. Judy said she had been writing since 1992, and Hilda said she had been doing it for many years. The majority, however, did it for the first time at my March 2009 workshop.

When asked what routines they followed when doing inspirational writing, responses varied. Some were already journaling every night. Hilda liked to go to a distant place to write, such as the mountains or the A.R.E. in Virginia Beach. Others, like Vivienne, claimed a quiet spare bedroom for her writing. Judy sat in her favorite chair and took out her calendar journal to verify the date, wrote the date on a steno pad, and began the writing process. Afterward, she drew a tarot card from the bottom of the deck as an indication of what to look for during that day. Some, like Maryanne, knew about using white light protection, calling upon their guardian angels and spirit guides for messages.

When asked to describe how they used inspirational writing and the messages they received, Hilda said she used it to keep grounded and record her thoughts for the day. Judy wrote for daily encouragement and said it was "like talking to a supportive friend." Maryanne wanted the writing to better her life experience and enable her to accomplish her purpose on Earth. Vivienne used it as a means to communicate with Mary Magdalene, but admitted she did not receive any messages she could decipher.

Bobbie was able to tap into the same Daemon that famous writers and composers reported contacting. She used the process to write a short story. "Over a period of two sleepless nights, I heard this voice that would not stop, and I was compelled to get up and write it down. It is written in a voice that is clearly not my style, and I had no intention of writing any story relating to the subject. I kept hearing the first paragraph repeated and repeated over and over until I got up and started transcribing what I heard. I have written poetry and other short stories from an altered state of consciousness (after meditating)."

Before beginning the first session, I recorded a brief welcome and explanation of the goals of the study, followed by a meditation to use before writing. My meditation included relaxation suggestions I had learned during my hypnotherapy training, which I also use in hypnosis sessions during past-life regressions. The technique involves relaxing the body, followed by a prayer of protection and instructions to confidently begin writing. I told the participants they could use my recording or their own meditation technique to get into a relaxed, inspired state in which the writing could flow. Most chose my meditation in the beginning, but as they became more confident, they started using their own music and relaxation techniques.

Once everyone was able to enter and exit a meditative state with confidence and ease, we began a series of exercises to explore different uses of inspirational writing. I wanted the participants to discover that this type of guided writing provided a perspective in an altered state that would have otherwise eluded them in a conscious state. I knew that profound expression of Truth is personal to the writer, yet it has the most power when shared with others, so I anticipated that the exchange of such insights would be a transformative experience.

The exercises consisted of four segments, occurring in monthly intervals. Since everyone agreed to share what they wrote with the other team members, I compiled them at the end of each session and sent them to the group for review.

Session I, August 2009

In this initial session, my goal was for the participants to establish a routine for writing, to get a sense of what inspirational writing feels like, and to know the Source of their writing. I asked them to focus on a generic, impersonal question—*"What is the one major lesson the United States still must learn in order to fulfill its destiny?"*

I suggested they write that question at the top of their paper or journal, or to type it if they were working on a computer. They were instructed to follow the guidelines I supplied for meditation and writing or to play the meditation I provided. After they entered an altered state, they were told to start the writing process, focusing on the question posed. I gave them two weeks to complete the assignment.

All eight participants sent back responses, which are shared here as I received them, with little or no editing. Their comments are in parentheses.

Maryanne

It needs to be free—free from hate, fear, and oppression. It needs to be free. It needs to be free. (Then I asked how could the US become free and could I help, I got:) My dear child, you are not alone to help with this. There are others who will help. My dear child, you must place your needs here up most hope. You need help on learning how to work with others. You need to find love in all things. You need to be majestic to see the whole beauty of the universe. It helps to be calm. It helps to be deliberate. It helps to be attracting love. It helps to be mindful of all things no matter how big or small. All things will work together. There is peace to be had. It is your destiny. It is there to be had. Go find love, joy, peace, and happiness for it is there to be had. It is there to be loved. It is there for all things. It is our hope to become one with all things. To find love joy and peace for all.

Poppy

Humbleness of spirit
Be gentle

Bobbie

Great power requires great thought and conscientious behavior. It is time for all great powers, and the US in particular, to see that they are but a part of a larger world. It is time to think with a world-view, which encompasses the great and the small, the strong and the weak, the rich and the poor. It is time to put aside the past troubles and turmoil and see with new eyes — a new world vision where all peoples interest are taken into account. The poor of the third world should share the bounties of the rich. The 21st century is here — a universal time — the US must be prepared to accept that change is upon us and move forward welcoming with open arms and hearts that which is to come. Thoughts of superiority must be put aside and equality and equanimity will prevail. A union of all nations, all peoples must be achieved. The US must cease to exist as a separate nation and the world — Earth will become one.

Cathy

Keep strong together
Anger management
Strong Mirror

Vivienne

Beautiful Nation Divine Providence Heroic Destiny of Promise to All
    Present
Spark of Knowledge
Heal of Soul
Sentiment of Gratitude
Powerful Energy Divinely Given Corrupted in Age
Dowse Fuel
End over End

Hilda

Let go of the conquering mentality, and let's flow with a feeling of love and caring. We must stop trying to conquer all that is out there. Let love flow and allow those to grow. Let's try and allow all persons to stay free and seek what they need to achieve their greatness. Unity is the word we must use at all times for the good of all humankind. Let's grow together and share love and contentment together. We must be united in our goals and seek out all that is necessary to find peace. Love is the answer. Let go of hate and unite for the betterment of all mankind. Let's flow together and find joy in our lives. Let's live together in harmony and allow all to seek their highest good. Life is too short to try and force all to become what you want. Let's all work together to create fertile soil that all children can play on and be free to run and play with a joy that fills them up, as their stomachs are full. May we all stay strong in our need to be free, but we need to do it for our good. Love is the answer. May it always be there, and may we erase our envies and hatred so we all can live in peace. This is supposed to be the land of opportunity for all who are on this earth. Let's allow all of us to grow and stretch as far as we would like to. May we all be there for each other so that life is tranquil and peaceful. Please let us love one and another and let all of us live with joy and contentment. Life is loving, and so let us live life in loving with a contentment that holds all of us together to seek all that is good for us and for all who walk this earth. In peace, let us be so no one is afraid but can seek their highest good. Love is the answer! Peace is the word! Caring is the wrapping of our souls to reach out and share it with all who are in our world.

Judy

[NOTE: Spirit often refers to her as "Lee."]

Dear One. Our Beauty. Our Joy. We are here to help with this project—but the project is bigger than you can imagine. A forum for the truth is needed. This will be a part of that. It will be shocking to some what comes out. The simple answer to the question is the Feminine Energy. The Knowing. Intuitive Connection to other levels and all others. The love and light brought thru the Feminine Energy. This is the lesson. Once that comes in, the connectedness is assured—the respect and caring of all is a given—a calling of the puddles into the flow—draining the water into the oneness. Vibration of the One in the all. It is easily pictured. Lift a board that has droplets and they all flow easily to the bottom—catching up with other droplets as they go—It is in the combining and the flowing that the power will build and build. No soul left behind. Prayers for the deceased and for the "outsiders." Prayers to cause awaking in the all. No one left behind. The grid humming with this truth of the all as one. Yes.

Lee. Our Beauty. Your time is coming. You have the pieces. You have the tools. Review and practice. You bring much to this time. Let your children find their way. They are safe. You are here for them. But your job, such as it is, is to be an example to others. Be yourself. Your authentic self. Your time is now. Practice and study. You are ready. You are here for a purpose.

As we have talked about before. The Polarity and Dichotomy is set up. Much has been put in place to Protect the Masculine energy. More will happen soon to Protect the interests of this masculine energy. It will be so shocking once uncovered that any future plans will be halted. Not by outside force—but by awakening of the persons set to implement. Pray for the Light of God to Awaken in each soul. That is the request. That God awakens in all. Lee. Our Joy. You are safe. This area is under the radar. The energy flows. Nature thrives and adds Beauty to the awakening. We are so grateful for your help and awareness. We are here and you are safe. Yes. Love, light, and laughter.

Jean

Hold fast as rock   stand steady as beacon of light, my light, for all

Spirit of liberty is my spirit   Open mind open heart   Trust Breathe my light   Guide love quietly   Build strengthening bonds of trust   Invite liberty   Show my will for creation

formed by Spirit for spirit

vigilance   remain True to purpose   Divinely conceived   Truth

No not   one   circle flowing on from beginning to beginning forever and again

unlimiting   not one   Truth   Beacon   Home   Light

As illustrated, about half received long, eloquent answers with complete sentences in paragraph form. These were written in the plural first person, "we"; for example, "*We* must be united in *our* goals . . ." and "*We* are here to help with this project . . ." and "*We* have talked about this before."

Cathy and Poppy received disjointed phrases, such as "Humbleness of spirit" or "Keep strong together." Vivienne wrote in run-on sentences consisting of disconnected words, such as "Beautiful Nation Divine Providence Heroic Destiny of Promise to All Present." Jean had equally disjointed phrases, but the manner in which they appeared on paper was interesting. The first word in the phrase was capitalized and the others were not, and each phrase was separated by a long space; for example, "Open mind open heart   Trust Breathe my light."

Hilda's message focused on love and peace, urging everyone to eradicate hate and to work together for the common good. Judy's Source focused on Feminine Energy being the answer and directed the comments to the writer, rather than to a larger, generic audience; for example, "*Your* time is coming. *You* have the pieces. *You* have the tools."

I compiled the messages and sent them to the group to review. I included a questionnaire that asked if they had learned anything new, if what they wrote impacted them in any way, and if it triggered any specific feelings, thoughts, and ideas.

Most participants said this was their first serious attempt at inspirational writing. The majority used my meditation, saying they found my voice reassuring and the music was helpful in their relaxation process. Bobbie said the Prayer of Protection made her feel safe. Maryanne preferred listening to an Enya CD. Others used their own relaxation techniques.

The bedroom was the most popular place to do inspirational writing during this first session, although Poppy sat in her family room, and Jean wrote at the kitchen table. Some preferred to work with natural daylight, while others worked beside a small lamp. All sought out comfortable furniture. Seven of the eight participants used a pen; Jean used a soft-leaded pencil.

In describing the process for this first session, Poppy called it "dreamlike." Both Bobbie and Jean used the word "natural." Judy described it as "easy and smooth." Maryanne said the writing "just flowed." Nearly everyone said the message came quickly, with words coming into their head that turned into sentences. Hilda described the process as letting her mind listen "and the words flow out." Poppy and Jean started the process by moving the pen in a circular motion for several minutes before the words appeared. Jean found this method especially helpful as it "served to further relax my arm and distract my conscious controlling thoughts."

As to the origin of the messages, Maryanne felt she was in touch with her guardian angel. Poppy called her Source a "Spirit Being or Eternal Consciousness." Bobbie did not believe they were "emanating from my natural thought processes, but from either somewhere deeper inside of myself or from an external, but connected Source." Vivienne, Judy, and Cathy said the messages came from their spirit guides. Hilda said "it is my Higher Power speaking," and Jean stated she recognized the "Voice" as her inner counsel.

Each participant said their handwriting was "pretty much the same" but added that the letters were either "smaller" or "looser" or "not as precise or as neat" as their normal handwriting. Most did not get a greeting at the onset of the writing, nor a farewell statement when the writing was complete.

The group was split in terms of whether they were surprised by their message. Those who were not surprised seemed disappointed. Poppy said, "I was hoping for something very different." Two said the message was not specific enough. Interestingly, Jean called this first venture into soul writing as feeling like an "ice breaker, a reassuring exercise," as if the Source of the writing knew this was the first of several exercises and wanted to establish a presence that felt safe and encouraging. Vivienne said she was confused about her message, wanting to know the meaning of a few of the phrases she received.

Most said they learned something they did not know before. For Poppy, it was: "I need to listen more." For Bobbie, "I need to trust and be open." Others said that this first attempt at inspirational writing increased their confidence in the process, especially for Jean, who previously considered this type of guided writing the "product of daydreaming or letting my imagination run free without consequence or validity." Cathy said the process proved "that I can really receive answers to a question," while Judy was empowered by the message that "they think I have the tools I need to do some good."

When asked if this session brought about a different

perspective—one they would not normally have attained in conscious thought—six of the eight said "yes." Jean and Hilda said "no," although Jean found the phraseology in her writing to be different from what she might normally express.

Participants were instructed to put their writings aside, reread them at a later time, and then report on whether or not their message took on a different meaning. Everyone did as instructed, but most said the message remained the same. A few, however, were surprised at how the message changed. "It was as if I were reading it for the first time and I had forgotten what I wrote," said Bobbie. Jean stated: "In rereading then and now, I can still discern an intent, but the feel and the sound aren't as full or light as I sensed during the process of recording. This suggests to me that I may have missed something."

Six of the eight participants said they practiced the writing technique before and after the session. When discussing the challenges they faced in doing this assignment, the biggest obstacle was finding the time to write. Poppy was frustrated; concerned that she was not doing something correctly or that she could not do it at all. Jean said the fear of failure was her greatest challenge.

Participants felt the experience of doing inspirational writing for the first time was valuable for them, both personally and spiritually. Maryanne called it "personally uplifting in a time of turmoil in our country; a message of hope." Bobbie took it to a whole new level, saying, "I find that I am more open to universal, 'psychic' quantum connections and the source(s) of consciousness itself." Cathy added, "It makes me realize how important [it is] to meditate and get in touch with my guides and higher self, and how much it could potentially help me." Jean stated, "I have gained a new confidence and approach to all unfamiliar or totally new endeavors. Whereas at one time, I may have gone out of my way to avoid dealing with something new or unfamiliar, I expect now that I will relish most challenges and their outcomes."

I asked for the group's reaction to the messages given to the other participants. Several commented that they found it interesting at how many of the messages shared a common thread.

When asked if the experience of this first writing session caused a shift in their thinking, seven of the eight participants said "yes." Many expressed feeling a sense of hope. Bobbie said it reinforced her belief that "we are all connected to each other and to everything in the Universe." Maryanne said the experience "enlightened me to the power of living our spiritual paths and how several living the pathways can make a great difference in the world."

Most said they would not change anything about the experience of this first session, with the exception of those who would have liked to have received a longer message. Looking toward Session II, the participants hoped to get more detailed messages. Some said they felt it was best to go forward without expectations. Knowing the question in Session II concerned soul's purpose, Maryanne said she hoped it would "jumpstart my spiritual growth," while Jean wanted to come away with an answer "that will positively influence my choices of life activities for whatever time in this plane that remains to me."

Session II, September 2009

In the second session, the group was instructed to meditate on a question that pertained specifically to them. The question was, *What is my soul's purpose?* They were to send me their writings and report whether they felt the guidance was in line with their soul's path or whether it provided a new direction for them to consider. If the latter, how did they feel about it? What new information did they receive? Did it change their perspective?

Again, all eight participated and once more the messages were delivered in different ways.

Maryanne

My soul's purpose is to find love. Love beyond expression. Love beyond birth and death. Love for others. To help others as if they were me. My soul's purpose is to find joy and happiness and by helping others you will achieve that happiness. First look to the outside to help others. When you help on the outside you also help in the inside. You have passion in you. You must use it to help others. Passion is full of love. Passion is fulfilled when you help others. For it is in the helping of others that you find yourself. Yourself beautiful lovely charming and compassionate. Love, love is the key to all things. Remember that. Love will get you everywhere. Love's all encompassing all powerful. It seeks you out – it is all around. Rejoice in it. Rejoice in the power of love. That is all now.

Poppy

grow
bring peace
healing
help show the way
instruct

Bobbie

The purpose of the soul is to seek the truth of your existence. Alternate realities exist, you are not alone. Trust yourself, you are on the right path. Seek to do harm to no one. All life is precious. Be yourself, express yourself, be grateful, be happy. Love freely and open yourself to being loved. This is just a test. More will come.

Cathy

Discernment evolution heavenly (I saw a picture of a white tulip) Agility crowning glory seeing the forest for the trees, behold dear one when I tell you truth, believe seek truth, trust, believe, be brave, mountains and molehills, hidden through the trees, seek, journey time travel, peace wisdom, forfeit guidance fulfill dreams goodness peace journey travel, gentle, gentleness, quiet reflection, knowledge seek, benign growth feel begin a new somewhere down the path seek wisdom travel to guide compassion strength seek joy, joyful giving energetically strings attached helpful. (Saw a hot air balloon) Beacon of light dimension wealth of knowledge peaceful giving time and travel seek, seek, fundamentally gifts show where being energy take wisdom to the highest realm soar spirits leap of faith begin nosedive lift up arms energy see clearly true vision clarity seek others peace thank you gratitude

Vivienne

Connection
Stars
Light
Touch
Unify Promises
Depth of Life
Birth of Life
Challenge
Rock
Beneath
Fire of Life
Service of Ready
Warmth of Gladness
Beneath Water
Saves

Trueness Heart
Gladness of Life
Wielder of Wind
Yields

Judy

Dear One. We have had this discussion before and it does remain the same. You are to teach what you know by example and gentle sharing. You are to use humor to shift energies and allow the truth to leak in. There is no must or should. You will always be at the right place at the right time. There is a calling to write and be seen—not the person but the truth to be known. It is easier than you think and the day is fast approaching. Lee. You do know how to move energy and cause healing to occur—but as you are learning, what is healing to one is not to another. By asking for permission you allow the soul to speak and most often prayers for Peace and love encircling the entity is what is needed.

Lee, Times are speeding up. This is time everywhere and with everything. The polar opposites are louder and louder and people/souls are experiencing much quickly. Many will surprisingly choose to pass over. You can help with that process since you know the truth about the other side. This is the time to flow and flow and flow. Let each passing be a minor blessing. Step out of the way of anger and heartbreak. God's love flows through you and all is well. Yes.

Love light and laughter. Yes.

Hilda

You walk upon this earth with a strength that reaches out to all humankind. The mountains are your abode and you can look down upon humankind. Your home is filled with those who love you and you share your wisdom with all. You have the power to touch and heal and your love fills you up with a sincerity that holds all in your heart. Your adornment is white and you bathe in a healing waterfall that flows down upon your abode so that you are healed with love and you reach out to heal all who come to be with you. You are so at peace and never feel alone even though you dwell in your abode alone. Your life is filled with the knowledge that you can help all who come to be with you. You walk with a softness that leaves no marks on the soil and yet you leave marks upon the hearts of those who come to see you. Your language is a language of love and compassion and you flow with a peacefulness that allows you to be aware of all the world. Your contentedness radiates out to all and the world knows you as Serene Lover who is touching all to heal this earth. Your days are filled with a caring that makes your heart fill up and spread love to all who are in your presence. Love fills you up and life is serene as you work to help others to share the love of all on this earth. You are an elder who only knows each day and no way do you reach out to the past or the future. You are filling each moment and the fullness warms your heart and allows you to breathe love and compassion for all on this earth; young and old, humans and animals, black and white, Latino and native, male and female, all vegetation, all who hunger, all who walk this earth. You hold all in the palm of your hands and the love that fills you allows you to flow with a restfulness that never ever takes your energy. Your white garb covers you with a love to share this love. May your pureness remain with you so that each touch spreads an energy of compassion and peace so that this earth flows on with compassion, joy and serenity forever.

Jean

To live. To love. To experience the Infinite. Grow closer to the Source of All to understand the connections and know that isolation is untruth. The tapestry of creation weaves many paths and many purposes and goes on forever. Be now confident that you are safe and are guided in love. Open yourself fully. Be not skeptical as you go but embrace.

Only six of the eight returned their questionnaires. When asked how this inspirational writing session differed from the previous one, many said it was "pretty much the same," although Maryanne and Vivienne said the second message was more personal than the first. Jean was less comfortable with the second message, but realized this may have been because the question was more personal in nature than the previous month's subject.

For this second session, half used my meditation while the others used a CD of their own or relied on their familiar process. None of them did it on the same day or time as they had in Session I, but nearly all of them did the writing in the same room, and all used the same writing instrument. Each said the writing physically felt the same as it had last time.

For some, the writing in this session started sooner than it had the first time. Jean and Vivienne said it took longer. Maryanne identified the source of the message as her guardian angel; Poppy felt it was "Supreme Consciousness"; and Judy said it was coming "from my loving guides." Bobbie stated that the words seemed to pop in her head, but added, "It was almost as if I felt them in my 'gut' rather than in my head."

As with Session I, their handwriting did not change, although Judy said it was a "little bigger than usual," and Jean claimed it was the same, "just looser."

This time, more participants received a clear-cut beginning and end to the message, although most still did not get a greeting or a farewell statement.

Most of the participants said they had a sense of what their soul's purpose was, so they were not surprised at the response they received when they asked that question. However, Bobbie said she was "surprised by the gist of the message" and was not sure what the last two sentences portended. Vivienne said she was a "little perplexed as to what it all meant."

Nearly all of the participants said they did not learn anything new. Some made the connection with their message to what they are currently doing and felt they were on the right path, but most did not gain a different perspective.

The majority said their message did not take on a different meaning when they reread it later, although Judy stated that the "responsibility issue suddenly seemed to speak louder to me." Jean added that her delayed reading provided a deeper insight.

Two of the six said they practiced between sessions. Most said they faced no challenges in completing the assignment, although, again, finding the time was a problem for Vivienne. Jean expressed skepticism and frustration, stating: "I'm just not sure whether this is real or just something I'm making up. Since my 'answers' lack specificity, I question their validity."

Everyone found the writing in Session II to be valuable both spiritually and personally. Maryanne said it helped to "guide me to stay on course." Expressing a similar sentiment, Jean said, "Though I was skeptical and frustrated in the process, the fact that I didn't just throw up my hands and quit is quite positive. It's so easy to just give up, but I didn't and I won't."

The group continued to be intrigued by the messages that other participants received. Vivienne found it interesting to be doing the writing remotely and wondered what the experience would be if the entire group were in the same room. Judy said it seemed as if everyone was "all on the same page . . . in ideas and concepts certainly . . . but even in wording sometimes."

Bobbie remarked that she found the different voices interesting, as was the fact that "some got long, beautiful, poetic messages, and others just get singular or small groups of words." Judy said she nearly cried at reading Vivienne's list of words and that Cathy's message "really spoke to me."

This session caused a shift in thinking for most. Maryanne had doubted the value of her work, but her message "placed the work in a whole new light for me. I feel like I am giving value to the world." Vivienne said that while the message did not cause a shift in her thinking, the process of being a part of the group as a whole had helped her in a personal way. "I find that we go throughout our busy lives and do things almost by rote and don't even consider the essence of who we are on another level," she said. "This experience has given me the opportunity to literally stop and smell the roses or stop and listen to the inner workings of my spiritual/ethereal self." Jean said the experience gave her "pause to reflect and realize how much further I need to go."

Session III, October 2009

In Session III, I instructed the group to open themselves to the fullness of Spirit and allow their Source to provide whatever information it deemed important for their spiritual growth at that moment in time. I suggested they word their question in basically those same words: *"What do I need to know at this moment in time that is important for my spiritual growth?"* I was looking to see whether this information came in the form of a personal message, whether it was a generic message pertaining to humanity, or a combination of the two. Again, all eight participated in this session.

Maryanne

Good morning. It is good to talk with you early in the morning when things are fresh. For your spiritual growth you are doing well, better than you have ever done before. We are proud of you. For you have lived many life times but your growth in this life has exceeded all you have ever learned in your other life times. You need to know love, love of yourself. You should love yourself more. It is easy to love others, but you have a hard time loving yourself. You find fault with yourself. You should stop that. You have done so well – have come so far on this journey. Loving yourself is the most important thing for you now. You are beautiful. You are kind. Relish in that idea. You can accomplish much with this knowledge. For all God makes is beautiful – remember that. For it is written that God loves all, sees all. He knows your beauty and is happy with you and your progress. You please God. Be sure of that. Just love yourself more and more beauty in the universe will unfold to you. Love all that God makes for it is good. The message of the universe is love."

Poppy

life is circles
meditation
patience in life is important
forgive self
meditate
peaceful music
beauty of nature
LOVE ALL

Bobbie

I am not of this body, only connected to it.

Cathy

Solace, peace, forgiveness
Troubles, battles
Keep focused
Try to maintain some judgment, because things aren't as they seem
    – put on a jolly countenance
Be cautious and careful, deception

Vivienne

Accentuate the positive in all

Trust in who you are in God

Whole presence

Virtue in everything

Grace and truth

Believe and hold dear those treasures and gifts of God

Never underestimate yourself

Guides surround you daily

Presence of mind to discern right from wrong and evil from Source

Believe with certainty

Gladness of spirit and soul

Recover your wrongs to path of knowing

Separation is false – Binding the Key

Struggle is over now

Battle lines drawn

Hilda

All things are there for you and you need to learn how to take each day as it comes. Find your center and dwell on it. You have the answers. You have the energy. Stop trying to do it all. Take one task at a time. Stay in touch with nature. Give yourself peace and contentment each day. Allow yourself to listen to the voices that dwell inside of you and know it will be ok. Stop stressing yourself. Be good to yourself. Walk along the beach! Climb the mountains! Walk in the park! Meditate each day! Slow down your heart and mind and know that you have the answers inside of you. Be good to yourself and stop making yourself feel guilty because you have not completed all your tasks. You need to reach out and ask for help and stop being so hard on yourself and stop being afraid you are not good enough. You have much to give the world. Just step out and go for it. You are a blessed soul and don't you forget that. Walk along the beach knowing that each step will bring you closer to the Almighty. As the sun shines down upon you know that it brings healing energy that will cover you with a contentedness that makes you know you are blessed. Stand tall and walk the path of peacefulness. Take a deep breath and allow the healing energy to come into your heart and soul and know you are a channel of healing that has a gift to share with the world. Let go of the human expressions and allow the spiritual phrases to seep in deeply to calm your soul. And So it is!!!!

Judy

Dear One, Our Joy, Our Beauty,

You are so on path and with us now. There is a flow that rushes thru you and brings more and more understanding and alignment. And it is in the alignment that the Good eases thru and in. Let it continue. Search out the Beauty and the Joy. The natural settings . . . the delicate art . . . the mighty vistas . . . the big and the small. There are real treasures hidden in the strangest places.

We caution you not to look back at memories or history of your current life—release and let them Go.

The fabric of this new world is made up of the beauty seen Now and beyond . . . the gathering and combining of the New Works. New Ideas. New Beauty/Growth/Creativity.

We promise you, you are safe and sure. The money flows. The body heals and many adventures await. Share God's love Everywhere with everyone. You have a gift and in exchange you will receive the magical understanding of the pieces into the whole. A new Quilt of fabric . . . Rich, textured—full of all the elements. MIXED MEDIA. We shout with JOY. You can see this.

MIXED MEDIA—That is where you live. A world of such diverse Beauty with each piece a part. Yes. Yes.

So now relax and flow—all is well. Your country will move forward. Pray when the spirit moves you. Others are praying too and the grid grows strong. Ignore the unpleasant. They truly will fall away. A great awakening is imminent. Yes. And soon. Time stretches and contracts. There are NO worries, it all gets done. Make plans and proceed. Seeds grow. Dreams evolve and only Good flows from these places. Magic Now. Yes.

Love light and joyous laughter. Yes. Yes.

Jean

Dreams will guide you. See beyond the mere surface actions. Record them as you waken. Record your feelings, colors, sensations. Reflect upon them throughout your day. Rise early to do this. You are most in tune in early hours. At day's end think upon the dream and write a lesson learned. Think also before retiring that you will state awareness of dream state. Express desire to know the way. As you practice each dream will give up its lesson more clearly. Keep the journal and look back for more insight. We are speaking to you and you are hearing us more each day. This is good. Your efforts are acknowledged and approved.

I sensed a shift in the tone of the messages the participants received during this third month of the project. The writing appeared softer, more loving, more empowering, and certainly more personal. The participants confirmed my estimation of a more uplifting message. When asked to compare this message to the one previously received, Maryanne said, "It was a message more of inspiration rather than knowledge gathering for me." Judy said it had "more energy and enthusiasm." While she admitted feeling resistance in past messages, Judy said this one started "more smoothly, and the message flowed more easily."

The participants seemed to wean themselves from my meditation, because fewer used it in this session. Some used a music CD. Poppy envisioned white and gold light surrounding her chakras. Again, none did the writing on the same day and time as they did the previous month. Every participant used the same writing instrument and all, except for Bobbie who was traveling, did the writing in the same place. Six of the eight said the writing "felt" the same as last time, although Judy said it "felt more energized and excited," and Jean claimed it was "easier, more natural" than last month.

Most participants reported that the writing started quicker in this session. Vivienne's comment—"It seems that it is taking a shorter time every time I do it now"—was indicative of the sentiment of the group.

When asked what was their impression of the Source of their message, some hoped it was from their guides or from angels but added they still weren't sure. Others were certain they were talking to their guardian angel, Universal Consciousness, or spirit guide. Hilda said it "felt like an elder was talking to me," and Jean identified the Source as a "deeper or higher level of myself."

Again, everyone said their handwriting was the same with a few minor differences; for example, "barely legible" or "a little sloppier" or "slightly more rushed." With this session, the majority sensed a clear-cut beginning and end. Most did not get a salutation or farewell statement, although Judy felt the beginning and end of her message was "a bit more elaborate" than before.

Six of the eight expressed surprise at the message they received. Bobbie's message was confirmed the next day when she watched a video of Deepak Chopra, "and he said, almost verbatim, the same thing." Jean said she was not surprised at the message but nonetheless delighted at its contents. "The question was 'what do I need to know,' but my message was what I need to *do* for spiritual growth."

Jean's experience is a good example of how inspirational writing can unfold in a completely different direction than anticipated. I believe this is because Source can sense what one truly needs to hear and zero in on that, regardless of what question is posed.

The group was split in terms of whether they learned something new. Those who said there was no new information tempered that statement by saying the message added to their understanding. "It reminded me of wisdoms that I knew but sometimes tend to ignore," Maryanne admitted. Bobbie felt "it validated what I have suspected," and Judy said her message was "more a confirmation." Jean stated that while she did not learn anything new, "I'm gaining an appreciation of the benefits of making regular time to attend to spiritual matters."

This sentiment was echoed when asked whether their messages gave them a different perspective than they would have received in conscious thought. Judy admitted that she was suddenly preoccupied with the idea of "beauty and creative pursuits" and said it was "an idea I have always had [that] has been ramped up by 100 percent."

Most of the group admitted not practicing the writing between sessions and fewer reread the message this time. Those who did practice said that the meaning had not changed, although Judy commented, "the excitement level is clearer." Time was still the biggest challenge.

Without reservation, participants said this session had great value for them. Maryanne said, "It helped me to know I am on the right track." Bobbie said her message "reinforced my belief that the soul is separate from the body, and we are connected to everything at a very basic level." Cathy acknowledged that taking the time to meditate and receive messages "could potentially help me."

In reading the group's compiled messages, Maryanne commented about how all the writings were positive. Poppy and Hilda said they were personally moved by Maryanne's message. "I am struck by the variation," said Jean. "On the whole, each message was in common with encouragement and support, but the flavor of each was as different as are, I'm sure, our individual personalities."

For this session, participants seemed less sure about whether their message caused a shift in their thinking. You can see them struggling with this question by the tone of their answers. As Vivienne wrote, "I don't know if it has really caused a shift in my thinking per se, but I know that the process that we go through each time defines my thoughts. Maybe it has caused a shift in my thinking, and I don't know it. I guess I'm just not sure."

When asked what they would change about the session, participants continued to express frustration that they did not get more details. Vivienne wished she could get "more definitive details instead of such short generalities, sometimes without knowing what they mean." Jean felt she was the one needing to change. She was hoping for "a lot less procrastination, more trust in the process, and follow-through in the inspired suggestions [would] make future sessions better and more rewarding."

Looking to the final session, participants were hoping for longer messages with more specific information and insights. Vivienne hoped it would be the "grand finale," and she would get the information she was looking for. Jean said that while it would be the last session for the purpose of this project, "it certainly will not be the last for me."

CHAPTER THIRTEEN

Soul Writing in Service to Others

Session IV, November 2009

In the fourth month of the project, I asked the group to meditate on a specific question of their choosing which had to do with their current life, such as relationships, careers, finances, health, or emotional or psychological issues. For this session, I wanted to incorporate the research methods of Sharon Van Raalte, as presented in *Transpersonal Research Methods for the Social Sciences*. Van Raalte introduced the idea of distant participation in the experience of the group as an interesting way to ascertain authenticity, not only for those participating in the study, but also for the researcher.

To apply this method to my research project, I read each participant's message individually; then using my intuitive skills and contacting my Source, I meditated on the text and attempted to obtain additional information on the participant's behalf. If this experiment were to work, then the information I provided through my own soul writing would embellish their message, providing a different, and hopefully transformational, perspective. If that happened, it would indicate that we both were tapping into the same Source—a sort of cosmic party line.

This type of "companion mode of healing" fascinated me, and it wasn't the first time I had engaged in distant soul writing. In the early 1990s, I had a past-life research organization called PLEXUS (Past-Life Exploration and Understanding) in Naperville, Illinois. One of our frequent guests was K. David Roell, a gifted channeler who had a big following in the Chicago area. After entering a trance, David spoke in a high-pitched, squeaky voice—looking and sounding much like Yoda, the revered and ancient Jedi master from *Star Wars*. He introduced himself as Dr. Fredericks—"Dr. Fred" to those of us who loved this delightfully witty character. Dr. Fred was an Akashic Librarian who had access to the Universe's record of everything that has ever been said, thought, and done. His readings were uncannily accurate, and I trusted his guidance.

During one session—and without so much as a heads-up—Dr. Fred announced to the audience that I was the clearest channel for "automatic" writing of any soul he had encountered and that people should come to me for readings. I protested, saying it was the last thing I wanted to do, but he insisted there was no reason why I couldn't channel information for the benefit of others.

That's all he had to say. I soon was besieged with requests to ask my Source questions. I reluctantly agreed, but after a few attempts, I realized my first instinct was correct and this was not the right medium for me. After all, I really *did* believe that all answers lie within. I was willing to teach the method to others but not willing to do it for them. I maintained that stance until I developed the final segment of my A.U. research project.

As stated earlier, conducting a soul writing session on behalf of someone else has never been comfortable for me. I consider inspirational writing as sacred work, and, in many ways, writing for someone else is counter to my belief that "all answers lie within." Nonetheless, in order to apply the distant participation research method to this project, I pushed through my resistance and trusted in the process.

At first I only was able to do one writing session per night, as I found the process tiring. The more I did it, however, the more energized I became, and eventually I was able to do several responses in one sitting. Of course, I had no idea how my responses would be received. I wondered whether my answers were going to be totally off base or whether they would add depth to the message the participants received. This especially concerned me when my answers seemed to go off on a tangent, and I questioned whether what I wrote had anything at all to do with what the participant asked. I was pleasantly surprised at the outcome.

The comments in parentheses are words coming from the research participants.

Poppy's Soul Writing

(Will the knee replacement surgeries be successful and fulfill and finalize this part of my spiritual path chosen for this life so that I can live a more pain-free life?)

pain is your journey
you can overcome
choose your path
new path
strong

show the way
choose
choose
journey
it is a journey
trust
end

My Source's Response to Poppy

My dear child, we are with you in love and in light.

From pain there often comes a knowing. The knee is the connection—symbolic of one on a path. Movement has been restricted because of pain and the wearing out of once fluid joints. Restriction has created new challenges—the question of how to get to one's destination when the way is impeded by pain—when one can no longer feel supported or capable of moving forward. It is then easier to remain stuck—to say it is no use—I cannot move forward. I am too weary. I have tried to no avail. Yet when the source of pain is indeed in the physical—and not in another realm—then medical intervention can indeed change the course. This is the case now—the pain is indeed a challenge but not brought on by anything other than a physical condition. You may ask—don't all physical conditions have their source in another element—in the mental, emotional, or spiritual realms? Is there a message such physical challenges bring to us?

There is—but in this case, it is not so much a message about some past issue but rather about what will come of it in the future. There is a before/after lesson here. Often souls in the physical must endure an experience in order to assist others through the same—a way to speak from a place of knowing—to allow one to serve as an example of what can be to those facing a similar challenge. Poppy is a teacher—but more of a teacher by example—an inspiration to those who know her. This experience will enable her to move to the next level and be a teacher, a model, to those who do not know her. In the *recovery process will come many truths that have eluded her thus far. When all is done—and successfully so—she will not only gain pain-free movement but will also gain new insights into what her new path is and where it will take her. From pain to glory. The way is long and difficult, but it is hers and hers alone to take. Many rewards await. Take care. This too shall pass. We leave you now in love and light.*

After reading my response, Poppy said everything I wrote was related to her message. When asked if it provided any new insights, she said, "Absolutely. It was much more reassuring and gave me a lot of comfort and reassurance." She said my message was "right on target" and felt it came from the same Source as hers but added, "You have a much better connection." My message gave her "comfort and relief," and she said, "It helped me prepare for the surgery and proceed with less anxiety and fear." She said the dual communication "reassured me that I have a connection I can access any time."

Saying its value was "very important" to her personally, she found it of "great value" to the group. "To see that even though each of us received [messages] in varying degrees, we all received, are connected, and can get answers if we only take the time to ask properly."

Maryanne's Soul Writing

(For my session I selected my career path. I work as a dietitian with cancer patients and lately I have been wondering about a career change. I love to read novels, and for years I have dreamed of writing my own novel. I have started writing a novel in my free time at night and weekends. Here goes [November 1])

Your career. You worry a lot about this because you want achievement. You crave achievement. That is your desire. We believe you are already achieving in your work. People are happy with you, but you yourself want more. That is where the problem lies. It is not really a problem but only in your desires. You are getting what you need – you want more, you want recognition for your work. You want people to look up to you and your work. That is what is lacking in your job now. You feel like people do not look upon you with respect for what you do. That is wrong. People do respect you and your knowledge. You are good at what you do even if you have your own self-doubts. Yes you are good at your current job and it supplies what you need. But you desire more. Now that is the rub – how to achieve more – we believe the book will work for you. Take you down new paths and open new doors. Do this along with your other job. Do not quit your job, not yet anyway. For you have a path to follow to get your book published and it will take time. First you must finish it then we will help you get it published. There is much to be done yet before this can happen.

(I did a second inspirational writing today [November 7] on the same subject.)

But you are good with what you are doing now. Why change? People like you there – you help them. They do respect you even though you don't think they do. You are here to help people and that is what you are doing at your job. You can find other ways to help you feel motivated and fulfilled. Writing – it is good for you for it uses your imagination and you enjoy that. Accept people for who they are and love them for that – that is key. Everybody has talents unique to them. Find that in the person and celebrate that. That is key. It has been a long and difficult journey you are taking in this lifetime, but you have learned so much this time. You have grown spiritually like never before. We are so proud of you. Continue down this spiritual path for there is still much growth for you to do. You still have much to learn. Love, everything revolves around love. Accept people for who they are and rejoice in them. Everyone can help you on your spiritual journey. Not just one person that you deem as holy like a minister. Everybody you meet has a lesson for you or can help you. Love, love, love that is the message of this earth. Love everyone including yourself. Look not at their faults but at their strengths, for strengths lie inside everyone. You call them talents. Whatever you want to call this gift, look for it, embrace it and grow from it. There is much joy left here for you. Look for it. Look for the joys everyday in your life and life will go better for you. For when you see only the good, more good will come to you. That is a promise. That is a message to spread to others, in your book and with your friends. Look for happiness everyday. For even when it rains there is happiness for you if you look for it. There is happiness in everyday if you seek it out.

My Source's Response to Maryanne

My dear child, we are with you in love and light. Maryanne's life parallels yours in some ways—that restlessness in feeling unfulfilled and unappreciated for all you do is common in both of you, as is the desire to find fulfillment through the written word. The Ideal is to find fulfillment in everything you do—even something as mundane as preparing a meal for your family, doing laundry or the dishes. To find joy in life's most simple activities will lead you to find joy in the larger accomplishments as well. For what is a task but an expending of your loving energy in a deed that has meaning? All actions impact the lives of others because you are all connected one to the other. With Maryanne—as with you—her actions are appreciated far more than she realizes, for few verbalize their joy at what she brings to them. Yet her loving service is discussed in circles at work and in the homes of people she interacts with—although those discussions are never shared with her. One never truly knows how they impact others—the extent to which their reach goes. It is rare for someone to say aloud— "I truly appreciate you; you've made a difference in my life." If everyone took the time to do that, the world would indeed be a better place.

It is for her—and you—to find the approval you seek within you and to know that God approves of you; angels approve; spirit guides approve. That is approval on the highest level. While in physical form, we understand the desire for human approval—that is the ego's need and a basic need for most people. But think of how your actions will be viewed on the other side during your life review. Do you not strive for your Creator to say—"Well done!"? That is what you must aspire to. It is not easy, but it is the way of the spiritual path.

As for a book, we would say Maryanne should write about what she knows. Write about her work and share her knowledge. Tell stories of how she has impacted people in how she has advised them and how their life changed afterward. That will be far greater read and benefit countless souls than a novel—although we would say she might find a way to tell her story in novel format. The focus should be on the message. Today it is foolish to give up a job that sustains you to follow a dream of writing. You know that first-hand. Many successful writers—like John Grisham—started out doing both, setting aside time to write each day before heading to work. It can be done. There is much Maryanne has to share. We applaud her desire to do so and hope she will follow her bliss in a way that brings her happiness and fulfillment. We are with you always in love and in light.

Upon receiving my response, I asked Maryanne if she felt the message I received was in response to what she wrote, and she agreed that it was. She indicated my response gave her a new insight, encouraging her to write her novel but to continue with her current job. When asked if my message touched on another issue she was dealing with but which she had not yet addressed, she said it touched on feelings she had about her current job. She was encouraged that my response suggested she was making a difference and that people appreciated what she did.

Maryanne did not think we were communicating with

the same Source but said, "It was like a second confirmation of what my Source told me." She added that my response caused her to pause and rethink her writing of the novel and that in the end, she agreed that her need to write was more to make herself feel more fulfilled than anything else. She found the value of the companion mode of healing as a confirmation of the correct way for her to go. She said it gave her a greater sense of connectedness to the Universe. She was elated to realize those on the other side saw her from within—"the real me and not the me that others on Earth see me as"—and offered her advice from that perspective. For her, the value of this exercise was the confirmation that she should continue with her current job and write for her personal joy. "In a way, that takes pressure off of the question of what to do once I finish my novel and makes the writing of it more pleasurable," she wrote.

Bobbie's Soul Writing

(The subject of healing, self-healing, healing others, group healing, etc., has come up numerous times this past year. I have been told by several people that I am a healer. My question is: Am I a healer? If so, to what extent should I be healing others, and how do I go about learning more?)

The desire to heal runs deep within you. You are a healer. You've been a healer not only in this life, but in many lives before. You've chosen a less direct form of healing this time as you have healed yourself of many psychic wounds and in sharing what you have learned you have helped others heal as well. These have all been emotional and psychic wounds that have been healed. The question now is whether you are ready to do physical healing as well. There have been times in past lives when your healing powers were not understood or appreciated. This caused great distress and is the reason you have thus far chosen a less interactive, hands-on healing practice. This is a karmic wound that you have carried with you into this life and is now being addressed. Meditate on this further and in doing so you can heal it and move on. You have witnessed the power of intention and group healing yourself. You are capable of doing this yourself. You are a healer, a natural conduit to the healing energy of All That Is. You are a healer, in inspiring others to be all they can be and reminding them they are loved, you help them learn to heal themselves. The power to heal others is within you should you decide to do so. The tools you need are at your disposal in the books and Internet, you have connections with those who can direct you and encourage you. Trust yourself. Know you are loved.

My Source's Response to Bobbie

My dear child, we are with you in love and light.

When souls speak of healing, they conjure up a definition that is ego-centered and not in keeping with the intent of the Creator for this wondrous ability. Therefore one must proceed slowly and cautiously when pursuing any kind of work in which healing is a part. In a broad sense, everyone is a healer. A kind word—capable of being spoken by anyone—carries healing properties with it.

There are those, however, who have skills that run deeper; skills accumulated over centuries that have been safeguarded in their soul's bank account of positive karmic attributes. Some use their hands to heal. Some their words. Some their movements. Some their mind. Others use the power of intuition, of meditation, of seeing beyond the veil through psychic abilities. While it is true that Bobbie has acquired more than her share of healing attributes over many lifetimes, she still has karmic issues she is dealing with that hold those attributes at bay. She senses her gifts and is eager to use them to their fullest, but she does not yet have the clarity to retrieve them. She must first think of her actions and how those impact others. Does what she does match with what she says? Does she truly walk her talk? Is she open to the words of others without judgment? Does she treat all in fairness and love to the best of her capability? Does she do unto others as she would have done to her? We are not judging—simply asking the questions posed to anyone who wishes to pursue their healing gifts. The answer to all these questions may indeed be yes. Only she can answer. If so, then she is ready to do the work to narrow her attention to the healing modality for which she is most comfortable and then to pursue that—and only that—with a passion she has never experienced before. Then and only then can she step out of the shadow of the past, observe the karmic issues she is working through with a grace that transcends them, and claim her role as a healer. There is a genuine softness in her nature that is nurturing to all who come to know her. She must be true to herself—recognizing her abilities as well as acknowledging her shortcomings. Seek forgiveness of those who have been wronged; forgive those who have wronged you; and—most importantly—forgive yourself. Then—with a humble heart—will you emerge in the fullness of all you are meant to be. We leave you in love and in light.

After I meditated on her message, the response I received was more direct and to the point than the messages I had received for the other participants. It had a sterner voice than I usually get through inspirational writing, so I was hesitant to share it with her for fear she would be offended.

But Bobbie felt my Source raised questions that were "very valid in light of the seriousness of my question." She said the information I provided gave her a new insight, adding that it "made me question the reasons why I asked what I did."

In terms of whether we were communicating with the same Source, Bobbie said it was difficult to say and to some extent irrelevant, adding, "I suppose that if we are all connected to one another and to All That Is, then the Source of both communications in the end is the same."

Bobbie said she "was humbled by the questions asked" and added that she would like to pursue the conversation further. "I am aware of a blockage in my energy system and no matter how I work on it, it still lingers," she said. "I have no doubt that this is due to the karmic issues mentioned. I'd like help in learning what those issues are and how to overcome them. I know that until I am healed myself, I cannot heal others."

Commenting on the companion mode of healing, Bobbie felt any form of communication—whether it is to self, higher self, or Source—is a healing modality. The message I shared with her affirmed her belief that "we are all connected to each other and a larger Source." In terms of personal value, Bobbie said my message was an affirmation of her belief in a Source, as well as a confirmation of a belief in her as a healer. As far as the value to the group at large, she stated, "I think each member will take away something from the experience similar to my own and to the extent that each participated."

Cathy's Soul Writing

(Question: Am I on the right path with my current career endeavor and will I have financial success? [The question was rephrased for her: Will I be a financially successful trader?])

3–5 years. Success teaches wisdom, gainful trying. Like a wagon (a covered wagon) that turns slowly, I'm making slow progress . . . hitting sand makes it harder to get through, but it's doable. Like the trip in the wagon, it's a journey - a journey for me, not just financially, but to learn more about me. There is no horse pulling this wagon - I have to power it myself. . . . (I see a covered wagon on a flat prairie). . . . There's open space ahead and no real obstacles, but I see great distance and vastness. I also feel my wagon is the only one there – I'm ultimately alone – ultimately I'm alone and must take the journey by myself – I can't rely on anyone else for help – The weather is nice and I feel comfortable, so there are no limitations on me, or discomfort.

(I feel they are giving me a picture of my current situation and leaving it for me to interpret.)

Right now the wagon is stopped . . . I'm going to have to push it to make it move and it's not easy because it's heavy and doesn't move easily. I'm stuck and I need to move forward to make some headway.

(They're making me answer my own question and trying to prompt me to see where I am. They want me to think about what I need to do to start moving forward again.)

My Source's Response to Cathy

We are with you in love and light. As humans, you have brought yourselves to the brink of what you call "financial collapse." This is an unparalleled time of transition. Everything you once held dear, believed in so strongly, is changing before your eyes. This is so apparent in the financial realm and is in so much flux right now that it is difficult—even for those on the other side—to say conclusively what will be. It is all up to you—to your free will—and the outcome seems to change daily. So the question about success in a field that is not stable is a difficult one to assess. The image of the covered wagon being stuck is an excellent analogy to your situation.

Think of what it was like for pioneer women. They had a vague idea of their destination—somewhere "out there"—a place west where they believed they would find all they were seeking—a new, happy life of limitless possibilities in an endless world of opportunities and rich land upon which they would build and reap the rewards for having endured such a difficult journey. So, too, is Cathy anticipating her future. Like the pioneer women, the future is not clear. When the wagon gets stuck, the women had to leave things behind to lighten its load so it could move forward less encumbered. So too for Cathy to do the same. Make an inventory of all the "heavy" things that are a burden and are impeding your progress. These do not necessarily have to be material objects, as in the case of the pioneer women. For Cathy, they can be attitudes, beliefs, feelings that are weighing her down and stopping her forward momentum. Being positive in what appears to be a negative time is most important.

What your mind conceives is real. Remember what Cayce said—thoughts are things. The mind is the builder. Remember this. Look into the wagon. See the box of negative thoughts and throw it on the trail. See how much lighter the wagon is now. Get out and push it. Dig the wheels out from the rut in the road. Remove the sand and through sheer will, nudge the wagon forward. You—Cathy—have all the tools you need to do this. Use every ability you have—your knowledge, your intuition, your wisdom. There is always an answer—always a solution, a better way. The road may be difficult, but it is not unsurpassable. It is time for creative solutions that only you can devise. There is no quick fix to a situation that took years to manifest—but for those souls committed to finding a solution—one will be had. We leave you in love and in light.

In reviewing the message from my Source, Cathy gained more information and encouragement. She felt that my Source took her message to a higher level and gave her clarification and guidance. "It addressed a broader issue with the financial markets," she said. "I hadn't really thought about that. I was mainly wondering as to whether or not I could make a success of it."

Cathy admitted feeling excited and grateful to receive more information. It gave her a "wonderful feeling of hope that my goals are possible, and a great feeling of validation—

that I had truly received information rather than having just made it up in my head."

This final exercise gave her "confidence that I can communicate with my guides or other souls that can give me information, and it is very empowering and comforting to know you have help on this journey."

In this assignment, Cathy's writing emphasized her feeling of being alone and having to do everything for herself. My response reinforced that no one is ever truly alone. It was this message that had the greatest impact on her, as evidenced by her final comments about this exercise: "I'll continue with the process [of inspirational writing] as now I have validation that I am receiving valid communication, and it'll help me along my journey—we're not alone! That's a powerful message— not that [I] ever thought we were, but I had never felt like I had any ability to communicate and now I know I do . . . That's a heartwarming insight. . . . Thank you so much for this gift."

Judy's Soul Writing

(This one got a little tricky. I worked hard at trying to get a question in the way you requested. But nothing seemed to fit in those categories; probably because I have been doing this for so long, I no longer really have those kinds of questions. Now that I understand how life works, it is no longer such a day-to-day mystery, so the only question I have is: How do I connect more consistently with Source, to hear answers [Truth] to all my questions? How do I maintain the alignment of my vibration [energies] to Source [the Truth] and to God's will? The recognition of the connectedness of the activities and events around me that form the bigger picture of which I am already aware. How may I serve to meet my contract coming into this life and to find the joy and upliftment of being one with God?)

Dear one, We are here with you always . . . all ways . . . yes these ideas are the only ones for you. All else can easily be handled and are not concerns. We know your impatience to be of real assistance and to get moving. But there is magic in the down time too. Real growth occurs in the quiet. You will never, never miss an opportunity to be at the right place at the right time. We help in big and little ways. And everywhere you go . . . you are acting in God's stead. Even in the quiet times when no words are spoken. You share your enthusiasm. You are a stranger who leaves a footprint of love. Yes. Lee, there is travel for you. And Healing work to do. These skills you have now could be honed. And discipline in the practice, but even a thought of sending angels is enough to aid the energy of the situation. Lee, it is not your role to help all. Each country, each situation, is demanding alignment of their own participants. You are shown where your energy is needed. And soon you will have resources to help many more. There is time for it all and it proceeds. Release here at home. Let go and step forward. Your alignment is maintained by the natural setting and rhythm of your world. Enjoy it all. We love you. Love light and Laughter . . . Yes.

My Source's Response to Judy

My dear child, we are with you always in love and in light.

Each soul has a path to follow, designed by them and the council that guides them prior to coming to Earth. While some come to know and understand that path, for some it is the unfolding that is the journey. How often do souls have an impact on others in ways they least expect and probably never know? Yet all acts, all synchronistic events, all meetings, all departures, all waves of the hand, nod of the head, smile across one's lips—all are recorded in the book of life. Expectations of one's chosen [path] are often greater than need be. The idea—I must be off to do my work—is often redundant, as the soul is already steadfastly doing its work on a different plane. Guidance is always abundant and at the ready. Each soul you encounter is never an accidental brush with humanity—it is with purpose and intent.

Have an Ideal and live by it. Do not allow yourself to be distracted by the endless question—what now? The silver thread to Source is not as fragile as one may believe—if you envision it always in your meditation, you can clearly see your connectedness at all times. There is an invisible veil that can be crossed so easily and is, by those for whom the veil has been lifted—it is for you and for she who writes this message for you. There is nothing new to be learned. It is already well known by you—yet there are infinite layers to that knowledge and ancient wisdom yet for you to peel away to get to Source. This is a gift you possess—to go deeper, deeper, deeper to the core—to that infinite, exquisitely divine light from which all flows. Once there, the understanding will pour forth in words others may hear and take in and then live through. You have done well—you continue to accomplish extraordinary explorations of the soul. Share this knowledge and wisdom more openly—find a way to say what is imprinted on your soul in a way that is tangible for others to absorb. It is a challenge many souls like yours are facing in these difficult times—but not unattainable by a seeker of your depth. It is yours for the taking.

We leave you in light.

Judy viewed my response as a gentle reminder that she was already doing her work, and although she felt the message from my Source was not anything new, she acknowledged that "the reminder to hold an Ideal was useful."

She felt we were part of the "same soul team" after reading the greeting my Source started with, "My dear child we are with you always in love and light." She said my response made her feel warm and loved, "like talking to a dear relative who I know cares about ME."

My response raised questions Judy wanted to further explore with my Source concerning the events of 2012, raising consciousness, and releasing the body—"some hard questions to ensure a full understanding of what is to come."

Like Cathy, Judy said the value this exercise had for her was the realization that she was not alone and that there were people with whom she could admit hearing voices who would not think she was crazed. "This process has very much made me feel like I am part of something so much bigger . . ."

Judy felt that the value of the exercise to the group was that the process encouraged them to more fully explore their connection to Source in a tangible way. She concluded by suggesting that we form an ongoing group with specific questions each month, something akin to an on-line dream group. "I would really like for this to continue, because I think the times ahead will need some clarification that this joint effort can bring to it."

Vivienne's Soul Writing

[Vivienne withheld her question so I was unaware of what she asked in her writing session.]

Admittedly yes, it is up to you. Focus on thought and go within for answers. Requirements not necessary to fulfill. Automatic outcome. Help and promise. Regard to all. Many will come. Reverse (then a squiggly line that is unreadable). Heavy notice of law. Bring together all. Notice of failure gone alone without you. Follow your hearts, dreams will follow always. Be alert on every day now and always. Forget and forgive. Thoughts promise to supply. Goodness prevails to you both. Weary times lead to quest of life. Be thoughtful.
from 'Beacons of Light' Thank you

My Source's Response to Vivienne

My dear child, we are with you always in love and in light.
For your new dear friend Vivienne, we would say that her role has

just begun. All that she has prepared for is now coming to fruition. As you have lit the light of Truth and shared it with her, so, she too, will light the light of Truth in others. She has been with you in many lifetimes. She was a part of the sacred circle of souls that traveled through time to be a beacon of truth to those who succumb to the follies of lies. This is why the Beacon of Light comes to her now. They have awaited her re-emergence for many years in this lifetime—standing by in the wings so to speak—until she was reunited with you and the others who will work together to dispel myths and mistruths.

She has that innate ability to see beyond what is in front of her. She intuitively knows what is true and what is not. She is an ally for you in a war against mistruths—standing steadfast by your side as you move forward with your work. You both are working on issues of freedom—hers in a different way than yours—more in the freedom to be and express her authentic self. Her heart is wide open, and from it comes forth the dreams that you both share. While you seek to be all you are meant to be, she will be there to assist—to provide sound advice and counsel as before—yet at the same time, not to lose herself in your work but to be an adjunct and to pursue her own area of specialty.

As yours is understanding the principles of reincarnation, she, too, has an area of study that is her specialty, and that is in the area of spiritual understanding—an understanding of the God force and how it is a part of all humanity. She understands the link between all living things—the continuity of life and the connection and harmonious relationship of one soul to the next. This is truly where her contribution lies. She should be encouraged to channel those truths more, and you can do that for her, providing her with the mentoring and platform she needs while she in turn safeguards you and your secrets from those who would use you to their own gain. In a world of adversaries, she is an angelic presence in your life, filling you with a genuine affection to enable you to feel safe and, above all, loved. We are with you always.

Because of the ambiguity of the message I received—and because we were close friends—I was curious what Vivienne's reaction would be to my message. She acknowledged that my writing was not in response to her message, adding that it was vague and on totally different topics. When I asked whether my response provided new information or insight for her, she agreed, saying, "Your response put a new light on some things I already knew, but hadn't gone as far in depth as your answer did."

She acknowledged that my response touched on an issue she had not addressed, which was primarily the identity of her Source. She said my response filled in a lot of blanks, "so it was very exciting to receive it from you."

When asked if she felt we were communicating with the same Source, she said there was no definitive way for her to know that for certain, but she was leaning in the direction of saying they were one and the same. She was elated with the information I provided. "It was your response that gave me a fuller understanding of why they were communicating with me and what part I played in accessing their knowledge."

Now that she knew the Source of her information, she had many questions and wanted me to do additional writing to find out how and when she would be using her spiritual understanding in daily life. She wondered whether this would give her a new path as a means to create an income. Was it something she would develop more, or was it naturally within her?

Vivienne agreed that this companion mode of healing was useful for everyone, saying she believed despair and disease could be healed by understanding its origins and by developing a sense of oneness and connection to God. "It is easy enough to believe that or say it, but to experience it puts you in a whole different ball game. You *are* the answers to your own questions and you have the knowledge to experience and determine the outcome of any circumstance."

As for personal value, my response showed her that we all had spiritual help available to us and that we could call upon it "to help us with our daily lives and communicate suggestions and solutions for our everyday experiences." Mostly it showed her that she was not alone and that we were all a piece of the same puzzle.

Vivienne felt the sessions had great value to her and to the group at large. "I loved it and would do it again because it put me outside my comfort zone, and [I] was able to reach out farther than I have before and was rewarded for that trust I put in my Source."

Hilda's Soul Writing

(My question: *When can I get back to myself? Do not like these feelings. Want to get on with my life.* I used a meditation that took me to the beach. As I listened, I saw Mom and this is what she said to me:)

You are cleansing and so just allow that to happen. I am here for you and so are your ancestors. We are surrounding you with love and we know how hard this is for you but it has to be. Allow yourself to experience it and know you will be a better person when it is over. I am here for you and I am so sorry I could not really be there for you when you were growing up. I had so much to deal with and had no way of knowing how to manage so I did not know how to reach out to you. I loved you but I did not know how to tell you and my head was filled with survival. You were my pride and joy but I would not tell you. I was hard on you because I wanted you to do better than me and I wanted you to have a good life. You have become a caring, compassionate elder and please know you are my pride and joy. I am sending you my love and want the best for you. Please know you are going to be all right. You will come out of this contented and wise. You will be an elder who has much to give the world. Stop being so hard on yourself. I know I didn't do right by you as you were growing up and even when you became an adult. I didn't share my love with you because I did not know how just as you are struggling with showing your love. I had a protective shell around me and I needed that to survive. I felt I had to be tough and I didn't want to get close and have you feel my fear. I am so sorry I did not let you know how much I loved you because I wanted you to be a strong woman and I was afraid you would not be able to hold up under the pressure. You were delicate and I wanted you to be strong. As I bring in all your ancestors, know that they are there for you. Nana is here. She always loved you and yet she only knew a little about sharing love with you. Gramma was old and only could share her talent of knitting. She is so proud you became a nurse because of her being sick. Here's Ida! You know she always loved you and was so proud of you because you completed the task she could not complete. She wants to give you a hug. Here's Uncle Jimmy. You know he always loved you but never knew how to give it. That's why he drank but you did know he loved you. Here's dad! He never knew how to express his love. Don't know why but he did care about you and he did want you to come and be with him before he died. He understands why you didn't come but he needed you and he wanted to say I love you. There are others here but can't spend too much more time with you. Oh! I must get Lin. He always loved you and is grateful you were with him on his last day on earth. He wanted you to stay but he wanted to protect you. I am here and I am content and I want you to know I am ok. Please stop being so hard on yourself. You will get everything done that needs to be done so stop being so hard. You are making yourself sick. Take all the comfort you can get and step out and know you will be ok. You are ok! You are loved and you are sharing love. Keep walking the path and take in all around you. Oh! here's Robert and he wants to give you a big hug. He wants you to know how much he loves you and wants you to be wrapped up in a warm comfort quilt covered all over with his love. He says it will be ok. You will be ok so hold your head up high and do what you feel good doing. You have many more years to go. I want to take away your fears and your apprehensions. Stop worrying! It is going to be all right. I LOVE YOU! Please hear me loud and clear. I feel I can say it now. Sorry I could not say it before. I LOVE YOU with all my heart and soul!!!

Hilda said that in writing this, she still wondered if it was her writing or her wishing this is what her mother would say to her. She added she was having a hard time and reading what she wrote she found many things were repeated, which only added to her confusion about whether this was just wishful thinking manifesting in the writing. She also seemed surprised at the length of the message.

My Source's Response to Hilda

My dear child, we are with you always in love and in light. The way of the truly creative soul is one of self-doubt and pain. One feels the hardships of life more keenly than others. One feels the exhilaration of life higher than others, and one delves deeper into the meaning of it all at a whole new level—and why? Because gifted writers such as Hilda (and you, dear soul) must experience the highs and the lows much higher and much lower than others, for it is at those higher, deeper levels that Truth resides. It is at those levels that the words exist to express in a new and meaningful way what the experience meant. You cannot write meaningful copy on any topic without first experiencing it yourself. Hilda has explored this realm more than you, as witnessed by the volume of work she has already produced.

Loss of a loved one, especially a parent, is a painful experience no matter how prepared you are. There is always that one conversation that was never had—all those questions that suddenly raise their heads looking for answers no longer at hand. Why? Why? Why? Your relationship with your parents brought up issues you are still dealing with—but it is important to understand this is a natural part of the separation process and is not unique to you [Hilda]. Therefore, there is nothing wrong with you—nothing you must address so diligently now. Time is your salvation. It provides a perspective that enables you to come to terms with all that is.

The messages Hilda received were genuine. They were not wishful thinking. They came from the people who stepped forward—not from her rich imagination as she suspects. She has a very large contingency of loving souls behind her. She speaks for them all now—truly taking her place as the wise elder. Women like Hilda have absorbed the wisdom of their tribes. Like the medicine women in a Native American tribe or other cultural tribal leaders, she is a vessel into which centuries of knowledge and wisdom have been poured, and now she is overflowing with the need and desire to share all she embraces as truth.

Hilda is a magnificent soul—a wise and great teacher who has a gift with words, words meant to heal, to inspire, to uplift downtrodden souls. She feels things deeply, and from that depth is where the inspiration comes. She moves people with her words and her actions, nurturing every part of their being. She is a most beloved soul whose work is far from over.

Fear not—dear one—for love is behind you, above you, beneath you—carrying you forward on your life's mission. Allow yourself to grieve. Allow yourself to feel. Ask for guidance from Source and your guides; seek the comfort from those who have passed but who hold you up in their energies that surround you always—and be about the work you are led to do. You are never alone. We surround you in the loving light of God, your Creator, who is with you always.

Hilda said the information from my Source was "right on the money" and that the positive nature of the message was what she needed. She was surprised that her mother came through and said that was comforting to her. She said the experience "confirmed for me that this method can be very helpful when you need some help in sorting out your life and your life's work."

She found reading the responses others received "fascinating" and said she felt this would make a good retreat workshop "where we can do this a few times a day with others responding to what we have written and having a chance to have a conversation with them."

Jean's Soul Writing

(What would you tell me that I haven't already learned or experienced in the previous sessions?)

You have always had all that you need to do anything you can conceive. Nothing is denied. That's free will. All is possible. Much distraction keeps you from believing and accessing all the treasures waiting for you. Put yourself in a quiet spot and trust what comes in those moments. Make it part of your daily living as sleeping, eating, exercise of the body. Approach the realm through exercise. Manifest. Reflect on even the smallest things because in these you will find the truth you seek. Though you choose to stand alone, know that others possess pieces of the mosaic of life. You carry pieces others use. Don't gather—distribute.

My Source's Response to Jean

My dear child, you are in the light of God so fear nothing.

For Jean we would say—beloved soul—you are the vessel in which the wisdom of many centuries resides. Few hold within them the knowledge that you have acquired over many lifetimes. With that knowledge comes a deep understanding of how the Universe operates—the harmony and spiritual understandings that are revealed to those who have taken the time to study the ways of the etheric energies. Each piece of the puzzle fits seamlessly into the next. It is of great value for souls to see the finished masterpiece that they are, yet to also see that the finished picture is made up of tiny pieces that alone are meaningless, yet when they take their place on the chain, when they fulfill the space allotted to them, they become a valued and irreplaceable part of the whole.

Seeing the movement of life from this perspective will give clarity to each soul. They will understand how valued they are—how they are not alone—how their contribution to the All That Is has importance and that without it, the chain of life would be disrupted. Each soul is important and cannot ever be replaced. How different each person would feel if they truly understood how significant their role is—how much of a void there would be without them. We are all part of the whole; a segment of the continuum that exists eternally.

The lesson of oneness is therefore your role—the idea that each soul has a part to play for the greater good of all; a mosaic of humanity that transcends anything that can be imagined in a linear world. In a place where there is no time, where there is no beginning or end, each soul exists in harmony and loving support of the other—all bound for the same destination, even though they may be on different paths. Illustrating this journey and the mosaic road that leads one on, is a portion of your soul's mission. You know what to do and how to do it—focus on this directive and record what messages come your way, until you see a clear path to your destiny. We leave you in love and light.

Jean said my input interweaved with her message as a "between the lines" missive. "It did not counter or contradict, but filled out, providing a bit more definition to the original thoughts I needed." She said my message provided additional insights to her soul's history. She said my message "incorporated a universal perspective; overlaying and reiterating the 'oneness' of creation." She sensed that my Source was familiar, "possibly a teacher or group of teachers," whereas hers was very close and personal. Emotionally, she experienced a sense of love, compassion, and patience. She wanted to learn more about her "wisdom of many centuries" and added, "I am driven by an overwhelming sense of hope, which may be the wisdom and understanding under the surface waiting to be assimilated into this life experience."

As a companion mode of healing, Jean said, "The mutual correspondence, or getting another 'take' on my message, provided me additional spiritual 'experience' and perspective and allowed me to extract more meaning from the message." She added that it gave her a greater sense of connectedness to the Universe and that the experience validated the inspirational writing process. She said that reading the composite sessions gave her a sense of belonging and helped her recognize that she is not so different from others.

CHAPTER FOURTEEN

Impact of the Project

At the conclusion of the four writing sessions, participants were asked to write—in a conscious state—how the process of inspirational writing impacted their lives. This included accounts of the process they used, the challenges they encountered, what could have been done to make the experience more applicable, what they accomplished, how their lives have changed, and whether they intend to continue the practice. Here are their responses.

Maryanne

Wow, has this been a wonderful, insightful learning process! My first experience with inspirational writing began with the class Joanne taught at an A.R.E. meeting. At the class, I did not get any writing, just scribble. However, I felt deep inside me that this was an avenue that would benefit my growth, so I continued to practice. What I discovered was that after I completed the recommended preparation of relaxation, cleansing with four deep breaths, prayer of protection, and visual imaging (I use one of climbing ten steps to Heaven), that the words would pop into my head. I started writing these words down, and they formed sentences, which led to paragraphs and messages. So that is how I receive my messages. I write the words down as they pop into my head. When I am done, I have a message from my guardian angels. I should note here that I do my inspirational writing with pen and paper, in my bedroom, usually early in the morning on weekends. This is the time and place of less stress for me and when I feel more connected to my spiritual side. I use an Enya CD for soft music. Celtic music I find soothing. All of the messages have been consistent and full of love and encouragement. I reread these messages often, for there is a lot of wisdom there for me.

I have to admit I was discouraged in the beginning with not being able to write the messages in a way that I thought they should come. When I allowed the messages to come by writing down words that popped into my head, it all became so easy. So my only challenge was letting my guardian angels come to me in the way they choose and not the way I dictated. What a lesson learned in not demanding my own way!

I think the questions asked in the lessons were very well planned out. The first one, I received an answer on how the country as a whole can be helped and then how I as a single person can help. The second question is one very much needed to understand my own spiritual path and journey—what is my soul's purpose? My soul's purpose is love, love of others and love of myself. The third question of what do I need to know to help with my spiritual growth was a great follow-up to the second question. Now that I know my purpose, what do I need to know to achieve it? My answer to this question was a message of encouragement that I am already taking the correct path and to continue this journey. This was a message I really needed to hear. It was a message more of self-love, an area that I need to work on. For the fourth question, I chose the subject of career, for during my middle age I find myself wanting change. Their answer is my current career is a good choice for me and my spiritual path, but I want to feel more self-achievement. Self-achievement is desired by me to help me to love myself better. I have started writing a novel to help with a new career path and my guardian angels encouraged me that this was a good choice for me and to continue it with love and enjoyment. (Interesting to note, they also said not to quit my day job!)

From these four questions, I have learned great lessons about myself, my journey, and where I should go from here. But I used my inspirational writing for other messages. I usually do it weekly and basically ask my guardian angels for new messages they want to tell me. Again, these messages are consistent and full of love and encouragement.

I want to tell you of one session I had in particular. It was going as usual when a new message or change in messages started to come through. It turns out that the message was coming from a person that I knew and who had passed away about a year ago. I was taking some spiritual classes from her before she became ill with cancer. She asked me to pass along a message to a mutual friend. This friend had been of great help to her during her illness, and she wanted to say she was sorry for not being nicer to her. She wanted to thank her for all of her help during the illness. I asked why she didn't go directly to this person, and she said that I had a special gift of receiving messages that our mutual friend did not have. She said I should develop this gift to help others. I passed the message along, and what a difference it made to my living friend! This felt good to be able to help two friends, and I asked my guardian angels if I should try to develop this gift as was suggested. They said I could, but cautioned that I could develop problems that I would not expect if I chose this path. This deceased friend came to me the next week and thanked me for passing the message along. I used this opportunity to get some advice from the other side. Her advice was to talk to my angels often and to actually do as they advised me. She also told me that my husband (he died suddenly in 2001) comes around me often but is unable to communicate with me because I have some issues to work out about his death. After contemplating this statement, I realized I still have some anger issues that he died when my sons were entering their teenage years and left me to deal with the problems. I thought I had worked through these feelings, but realized that I just hid them deep inside without resolving them. I have asked my guardian angels if my husband still comes around, and they assure me that he comes often and extends his help from the other side to both my sons and me.

One scary thing has happened to me with the inspirational writings. One time I was starting a session, and my angels told me to stop because an evil spirit was around. I stopped right away, and I have to say that for about two weeks after that, I felt really down and depressed. But that did pass, and I am back to communicating with my angels again.

I think this shows how inspirational writing has helped me stay on track. I would like to add that the comfort I get from the uplifting messages from my angels helps me to stay upbeat and be able to better live my purpose of love. I think this is an excellent example of starting a project to help another and in return receiving a wonderful gift. I definitely plan to continue with inspirational writing.

Bobbie

As I look back on the last few months of participating in this project, the first thing that comes to mind is a feeling of gratitude in being able to participate, knowing that my efforts helped someone else achieve an important objective. My next thought is feelings of personal accomplishment, success in completing a goal, delving into new territory, and finding answers.

So what have I learned? Maybe I shouldn't say I learned—it is more that I received confirmation of a number of things that I already knew or believed. First, the answers to all of my questions are available to me, if I question with an open heart and an open mind and trust the answers I receive are the right ones for me. I knew this from working with my dreams and meditating. This experience showed me another path to the same goal. Second, that I am a healer (we all are) and have been for many years, but in an indirect way—through sharing my experiences and encouraging others to not be afraid of learning the truth about themselves, primarily through my writing and my Notes from a Dreamer website (www.notesfromadreamer.com). I also suspected that I am working through a karmic issue that I must play out before I can be the best I can be. Third, we are all connected—to each other, to everything in the universe, and to one Source or Consciousness.

It was interesting to read the messages received from different people—how some were long, very personal and drawn out, while others only received words or short phrases. That is, except in the final session, when everyone's answers were complete sentences and paragraphs. Perhaps because the last question was truly a personal one, they required (deserved) more detailed, complete responses?

Each session for me seemed a little different. In some I received immediate responses, others took longer. I did some in the afternoon, some late evening, and others still later—as today, early morning. I listened to Joanne's meditation beforehand on some, and on others I only meditated. I used a plain old ballpoint pen and paper for each assignment. I think it became a more natural process with each new experience, and I probably will try it again in the future when I am truly lost for an answer.

How has my life changed? Well, I am giving more serious thought to different healing modalities to see which one suits me best.

Judy

I have been doing this writing since April 1991. What I found most enlightening about this exercise, working with a group, and doing specific questions . . . was the fact that specific questions can get specific answers. . . . It had never occurred to me before to ask about specific things. . . . Mostly I do a daily session where I sit down and write whatever they say to me at the time. . . . Often it has elements of things I have been thinking about, either as a main focus or as a small aside. But it never occurred to me to be specific and direct the flow.

I loved reading the results the others got to each exercise. I could readily see the thread and continuity between each writer's words. Often I felt that their inspiration was coming from my own personal guides. Many times I felt the love so strongly of being cared for and accompanied by loving beings, that I was overwhelmed with emotion. Their messages seemed to be for me as well.

I will continue to do this writing because it is an integral part of my spiritual practice. (It is nice to know I have friends in high places, so to speak.) What I would find help-ful and enjoyable is if this group experience could continue . . . rather like a dream group. Working on one specific issue and sharing the answers with the group . . . being given more specific questions . . . to stretch us to get specific information . . . thus proving to ourselves that we have this psychic ability and assistance.

This experience is a door opener . . . that is extraordinary in its potential. . . . I think as a group, we just inched the door open a little . . . as a group we may be able to open it completely.

Jean

Over the past months, through the use of inspirational writing, I believe that my self-imposed intellectual and spiri-tual boundaries have expanded significantly. I don't doubt that this expansion overflows into my physical realm also.

For the most part, I followed the guidelines provided in the guidebook, and particularly the tape, to conduct my writ-ing sessions. It was only in the last that I diverged. Instead of using the tape, I guided myself through the relaxation steps in quiet, without music or other sounds. My surroundings are very quiet and serene, so I did not experience difficulty achieving the appropriate state of relaxation. Throughout all the sessions, my sense of "hearing" the message was much like tuning in to an on-going conversation. I didn't experience greetings or farewells. The only difference I would describe between ordinary random thoughts running through my mind and the messages received during the sessions, was that the messages stayed on point until completion, whereas my usual random thoughts run the gamut of subjects, frequently just incomplete snatches of ideas. The physical process of writing probably facilitated the focus.

After each session, I would read the compiled participant writings with relish because there would invariably be some insight or perspective that would trigger a new thought process or attitude in me. The uncertainty and lack of confidence in the process I felt as I attempted my first writing faded in the subsequent sessions because I recognized the commonality of the experience expressed in the others' writings. I particularly appreciated the final session with the feedback response. This was extremely beneficial to me, and I think it would be for every beginning inspirational writer. If a resource, like a network of inspirational writers, exists, I would like to participate to receive and provide others feedback responses.

The biggest challenge I faced during this process of inspirational writing was tuning out all the "noise" in my head so that I could "hear" the message. I found doubts to be the loudest offender, but as I stated above, the sense of commonality I gained from the writing of the other participants helped a lot to quiet them. Repeating the process for each successive session, I found my experience more sure and comfortable. I do intend to continue practicing inspirational writing because I find the counsel reassuring in these very turbulent times. Taking time to be still regularly, to converse with the Creative Forces, I think will be one of the most effective activities I can make part of my daily life for improved mental, physical, and spiritual well-being.

As for a suggestion to make the experience more applicable, I think some additional feedback responses might be included, possibly for the group as a whole, on impersonal questions, and/or individually on the ones that were more personal. I can't overstate how valuable I felt the feedback response to be. For me, it provided validation and a rounding out of the whole experience.

Cathy

The project of the inspirational writing was a wonderful experience for me. I started out not having experienced any inspirational writing before, to learning how to do it, to finally having some success with it. In the beginning, I had a hard time learning to relax, let my mind calm down, and receive the messages. It started with just some words here and there, and not feeling like I was really getting much information. The next time, I found it a little easier to relax and let my mind tune in, and each time it got a little easier. Each time I seemed to get more information and instead of just a word here and there, it seemed to come in phrases. By my last assignment, I was feeling more connected, and the information was coming more easily and more completely. By the third assignment, I had started to get some images, and by the last one, I got several clear images. And pretty clear messages. I really felt the message was coming from a Higher Source and that it was helpful information.

When your message confirmed the information that I was getting, it really gave me confidence in my ability to communicate—that I wasn't just making it up! And it was *very helpful* information that I am taking to heart and working on! I want to continue the inspirational writings now that I know I can do it. I feel that the guidance I can receive will be very useful, and it's so comforting to know that our guides are able to help us and that we can access our higher selves through this process. It's *very* exciting to know that we *all* have the ability to do this!!

Poppy

I wish I had been one of the ones who received long, direct messages. I know that I was receiving, though, and that was and is exciting and empowering. Each time I would go into meditation for this—at a certain point, my greyhounds would make a fuss, whether they were with me or in a different room—I would have to reassure them and then go deeper again.

It is empowering to know that I can always ask if I have a question and that I will get something to guide me. I really enjoyed reading everybody's responses each time. It made it more meaningful. Joanne's reading on the last question for me personally was very important and helpful for me.

Hilda

The deepest experience for me was the message I received from my mom, which meant a lot to me because it was sooooo comforting and made me realize that she did care but was unable to share that with me.

Vivienne

Having agreed to be part of the process for this Inspirational Writing "class," I set out to find out definitively from whom, what, or where it was that my writing originated. I was keen to let these writings define who I was as I walked this path on Earth. What I found was a method that worked for me that may not work for others.

In the beginning of the sessions, I tried to keep the pen in direct contact with paper at all times so that I could let my Source or Influence guide the pen, rather than *me* guide the writings. I found that it was more of an effort to sense what was guiding me, or rather the pen, to write. When I got to the third session, I realized that those words or phrases that came to the front of my mind without my guidance seemed to be more of an "inspiration" of words or thoughts and felt led, almost compelled, to put them to paper. This same process was used with the last, or fourth, session, and I felt as though I was opening the gates wide open where once I only deemed to stand and hope for inspiration to come to me.

I realized that this Source or Knowing is with me always; however, I have not always been open to receiving. This whole process permitted me the *allowing* that has always been necessary to move forward. Without my *allowing*, I have only been moving on the periphery of this inspiration or knowing. It was as if a light went off in my head, but more importantly my heart and soul, *that* part of me that *knows* this is the way the process should proceed in the future in order to get the biggest bang for my spiritual buck. It felt as though I've always known and understood this Source, but hadn't been willing or able to put all the pieces together till this course.

Things don't just "happen" in life; we meet someone or go someplace, and you feel that this is the way it's always been. This class has given me the impetus and momentum to not only *want* to continue on with the inspirational writing, but leads me to wonder what magical things could be offered up to me in the future. I take nothing for granted, and the world, this and all the others, truly *is* my oyster. I am anxiously waiting to read or hear my inspirations and hope that they will work in a way that is helpful to not only myself but to others as well.

Chapter Fifteen

Reflections

When I first began doing soul writing, I had no idea that it was a powerful tool of transformation. Like many novice writers, I was clueless about what a tremendous gift we have been given. I did not stop to think about all the ways it could be used—from seeking answers to everyday questions about finances, relationships, careers, and health issues to those dealing with esoteric philosophical issues, such as soul's purpose, past lives, Universal Laws, and dreams. That did not come until years later when I took what had been a "hobby" for me and actually looked at it from a higher perspective.

When it finally sunk in that soul writing is a method of channeling information from a Higher Source and that information can be applied to all aspects of life, I was as awestruck as I was confused. It just seemed too easy. There had to be more to it than meditating and applying pen to paper. If the process of communicating with Source was not reserved for a handful of select souls, but instead something that everyone can learn and successfully accomplish, why wasn't everyone doing it?

Time and time again, this question comes up during my workshops. People are astounded that they get something on the first try. Each time I invite members of the audience to share what they received, inevitably one brave soul stands and reads a message that touches everyone in the room. This is usually when the tissue box is passed around.

How incredible to know that this tool of transformation gives us the ticket to travel to that platform where we can tap into the collective consciousness and get answers to any question we pose. Imagine that—*any question we pose*. Cayce said we have access to the answers to those questions through meditation and inspirational writing.

During the course of this research project, I watched in amazement as a group of eight women made the journey from knowing little if anything about inspired writing to being able to identify and connect with their Source and develop a loving relationship in which guidance was provided through the written word. In a very short amount of time, they discovered how this method enriched their lives, as evidenced by the guidance they received on both generic and personal issues.

Everyone agreed that soul writing resulted in a personal and spiritual transformation. They overcame their doubts and gained confidence in their ability to connect with and trust the guidance from their higher self. They also came to feel a growing connection to the others doing the writing. Despite the fact that none of the participants met during the course of the project, they nonetheless developed a spiritual camaraderie based only on reading each other's messages. An undeniable connection developed during the course of the project, not only with each other, but with every other spiritual being occupying a physical body. They discovered a link to every other soul and realized there was no separation between us; we all came from the same Source, were nurtured by the same Source, and would return to the same Source.

It was a humbling experience for me to know that I helped guide them to this discovery. It is sometimes difficult for me to absorb the fact that what started as a childhood game under my parents' bathroom sink became my soul's work nearly fifty years later. I wonder now what I would have done with this incredible gift had I known I possessed it all these years. I think about how life altering it would be to introduce the process of guided writing as early as elementary school. If we could teach our children how to put down their electronic devices, close their eyes for some quiet time, slow down their thoughts, and put their pen to paper, imagine what wonders they would discover as they explore the depths of their own inner being. How many young people do that? For most, external stimulation is what life is all about. What if we took the time to show them that there is a wealth of knowledge, of creative and unique methods of expression that are waiting to burst forward? The world would be a very different place. Who knows? That just might happen.

Resources

Baldwin, Christina. (2007). *Life's Companion: Journal Writing as a Spiritual Practice.* New York, NY: Bantam Books.

Braud, William, and Rosemarie Anderson (eds.). (1998). *Transpersonal Research Methods for the Social Sciences: Honoring Human Experience.* Thousand Oaks, CA: Sage Publications.

Cameron, Julia. (1995). *The Artist's Way: A Spiritual Path to Higher Creativity.* New York, NY: G. P. Putnam's Sons.

Cayce, Edgar. *Edgar Cayce Readings.* Virginia Beach, VA: Edgar Cayce Foundation.

———. (1992). *A Search for God.* Virginia Beach, VA: A.R.E. Press.

Cayce, Hugh Lynn. (1964). *Venture Inward.* New York, NY: Harper & Row.

Conner, Janet. (2008). *Writing Down Your Soul: How to Activate and Listen to the Extraordinary Voice Within.* San Francisco, CA: Conari Press.

Couturier, Andy. (2005). *Writing Open the Mind: Tapping the Subconscious to Free the Writing and the Writer.* Berkeley, CA: Ulysses Press.

Harman, Willis, PhD, and Howard Rheingold. (1984). *Higher Creativity: Liberating the Unconscious for Breakthrough Insights.* Los Angeles, CA: J. P. Tarcher.

Knoche, Grace F. (1988). "The Secret Doctrine of the Ages." *Sunrise Magazine.* Pasadena, CA: Theosophical University

Press. Retrieved January 10, 2010 from www.theosociety.org/ pasadena/sunrise/37-87-8/th-gfksd.htm.

Michele, Desirée. (2006). *Enhance Your Psychic Abilities through Automatic Writing.* Sedona, AZ: Infinity Books.

Mühl, Anita M. (1930). *Automatic Writing.* Dresden and Leipzig, Germany: T. Steinkopff.

New World Encyclopedia contributors. (2008). "Automatic Writing." *New World Encyclopedia.* Retrieved January 7, 2010 from www.newworldencyclopedia.org/entry/Automatic_writing ?oldid=678091.

Pennebaker, James W., PhD. (1997). *Opening Up: The Healing Power of Expressing Emotions.* New York, NY: Guilford Press.

Psychic 101 contributors. (ND). "Automatic Writing." *Psychic 101.* Retrieved January 8, 2010, from www.psychic101.com/ automatic-writing.html.

Reed, Henry, PhD. (2007). *Channeling Your Higher Self.* Virginia Beach, VA: A.R.E. Press.

Schucman, Helen, PhD. (2007). *A Course in Miracles.* Mill Valley, CA: Foundation for Inner Peace.

Sellers, Heather. (2009). "The Value of Writing by Hand." Retrieved January 11, 2010 from http://joycastro.com/2009/06/the-value-of-writing-by-hand-q.html.

Sutphen, Dick. (1988). *Automatic Writing.* (VHS Recording No. 131). Malibu, CA: Valley of the Sun Publishing.

Tymn, Michael. (2007). "Automatic Writing: Like Holding a Live Bird." Retrieved September 2008 from http://metgat.gaia .com/blog/2007/8/automatic_writing_like_holding_a_live_ bird.

Van Praagh, James. (2001). *Heaven and Earth: Making the Psychic Connection.* New York, NY: Simon & Schuster.

Walsch, Neale Donald. (1997). *Conversations with God: An Uncommon Dialogue,* book 2. Charlottesville, VA: Hampton Roads Publishing Company, Inc.

Wikipedia contributors. (2008). "Automatic Writing." Retrieved August 2008 from http://en.wikipedia.org/wiki/Automatic_ writing.

About the Author

Born and raised in Chicago, Illinois, Joanne DiMaggio is a graduate of the University of Illinois/Chicago Circle Campus with a B.A. in history. Joanne earned her masters degree in transpersonal studies through Atlantic University in Virginia Beach, Virginia, in May 2010. Her culminating project (thesis) was on inspirational writing and served as the basis of this book, *Soul Writing: Conversing with Your Higher Self*.

Joanne has been actively involved with Edgar Cayce's Association for Research and Enlightenment (A.R.E.) since 1987. In 1990, she became one of the founding members of the A.R.E. Heartland Region, and she has been the coordinator for the A.R.E. Charlottesville, Virginia, area since August 2008.

A freelance writer with a background in marketing and public relations, Joanne worked in the Chicago media market for many years until moving to Charlottesville in 1995. During her long career, she has had hundreds of articles published in newspapers and magazines.

Soul Writing Workshops and Classes

Are you interested in having Joanne personally guide you through the soul writing process? Joanne conducts onsite Soul Writing Workshops to interested groups for either a half-day, full-day, or weekend retreat. She also offers a month-long, online course in which she works one on one with the participant. This course includes guided meditations and four different soul writing exercises, plus downloadable materials and lectures.

For information on workshops or classes, visit:

www.soulwriter.net.

Spirit Song is a line of greeting cards written by Joanne DiMaggio using soul writing. Each card is designed to uplift body, mind, and spirit, harmoniously blending black-and-white nature photography and self-empowering messages. These cards are produced on exceptionally high quality paper that visually portrays the verse, elevating the cards to more of a fine art piece than a casual greeting card. This marriage of photo and verse is one of the unique aspects of the cards. The nature scenes and outside quotation set up a mood which blossoms on the inside with one of Joanne DiMaggio's original verses written through soul writing. Because of the profound verse and artistically inspired photographs, those seeking a more spiritual, universal message when conveying sympathy, joy, encouragement, or friendship truly appreciate these cards.

These cards are $1.95 each or a packet of five for $8.75, including shipping and handling. Order them individually or get a packet of five containing one of each card or five of one card.

90-001

*Death is but a temporary transition
from this world to the next.
Know in your heart that
you will be together again . . .
To laugh . . .
To cry . . .
To love.
As you have before,
so you will again.*

90-002

*You have it within you
to achieve a greatness
limited only by the
boundaries of your
belief in yourself.*

I believe in you.

90-003

And you, my friend, I have
known before.
In countless ages past.
In the great light of God.
Through adversity and sublime
I have known you
as I know you now.
In love
and in Light.

90-004

Are we not all one
part of a greater force
from which stems all creation?
Share in that which is your
birthright.
Rejoice in the magnificence of
the dawn.
And know you are of it all.

90-005

A bright warm sky
is burning in your heart.
No need to search outward.
No need to look out.
Be as one with sky and wind,
but know all answers
lie within.

Order by mail by sending a check to:
Olde Souls Press, LLC
P.O. Box 6475
Charlottesville, VA 22906-6475
Or online at www.oldesoulspress.com using Pay Pal